Unlocking Leadership
Potential at Every Level

BREAKING BOUNDARIES

ROBERT D. MURPHY

CRYPTO FLIGHT

Published by Crypto Flight LLC

For more information, contact: hello@cryptoflight.io

ISBN (electronic book): 979-8-9874420-3-6
ISBN (print):   979-8-9874420-2-9

Table of Contents

Dedication

To my dad, Bob Murphy—your courage has always challenged me to push beyond the safety of the runway, teaching me that the greatest growth comes from navigating uncharted skies.

Introduction

"Do not wait; the time will never be 'just right.' Start where you stand, and work with whatever tools you may have at your command." – Napoleon Hill

In today's competitive work environment, the path to career success is rarely as straightforward as it seems. Most professionals believe that hard work alone will earn them the next promotion, the next opportunity, or the next phase of growth. But the truth is far more complex—and far more empowering once you understand it. The roles you aspire to, the promotions you want, and the recognition you crave don't just happen because you "do good work." They happen when you *break boundaries*— when you understand how to strategically position yourself within your organization, build trust with the right people, and consistently deliver results that align with the broader goals of your company.

This book isn't about generic career advice. It's about mastering the subtle art of career progression by leveraging influence, understanding the psychology of relationships, and knowing how to take control of your professional destiny. If you're stuck in a role, plateauing without knowing why, or struggling to make a strong case for your next promotion, *Breaking Boundaries* will show you exactly what you're missing.

Over the past 20 years, I've navigated my way into leadership positions at every company I've worked for—not by accident, but by understanding the mechanics of career advancement. I've learned that influence is built not through title, but through trust. Consistency in delivering results isn't just a personal achievement; it's how you become indispensable to those around you, whether they're peers or decision-makers.

THE MYTH OF THE NEXT PROMOTION

One of the greatest misconceptions professionals have is thinking they know what the next role entails, or worse, believing they are entitled to it simply because of tenure or effort. Promotions don't materialize because you clocked in the hours; they materialize when you understand the role itself—its responsibilities, challenges, and contributions to the organization. More importantly, promotions happen when you demonstrate that you're already operating at that next level through your actions and relationships.

In my earlier work, *Leadership with a Purpose*, I delved into the challenges leaders face, how to find your place as a leader, and how to differentiate yourself in complex situations by applying practical skills at the macro level. *Breaking Boundaries* takes those concepts further, offering a unique perspective on how to use psychology and your influence on those around you—whether they are senior or junior—to create opportunities for career growth. In this book, I will teach you how to take control of your career by understanding the key players in your organization and their goals, learning to play the game ethically, and positioning yourself as a trusted partner in the success of others.

A REPEATABLE FRAMEWORK FOR CAREER SUCCESS

This isn't a book filled with leadership clichés or abstract theories. It's a step-by-step guide to using your current role as a launchpad for future success. You'll discover how to identify the functions of those around you, how to build relationships based on trust, and how to create sustainable career growth. This approach is not a one-time fix—it's a repeatable framework you can apply at every stage of your career to achieve consistent advancement and influence.

Leadership isn't just about holding a title; it's about creating opportunities for yourself and others. By the end of *Breaking Boundaries*, you'll know how to wield your influence—whether you're managing a team, reporting to senior leadership, or working alongside your peers—to shape not just your career, but the careers of those around you.

WHO THIS BOOK IS FOR

This book is written for the ambitious early- to mid-career professional who is eager to fast-track their growth. If you're tired of waiting for the next opportunity to "just happen," and you're ready to take deliberate action to create your future, *Breaking Boundaries* will arm you with the insights and tools to break through the barriers holding you back. Whether you're plateaued in your current role or simply striving to be the best you can be, the strategies in this book will equip you to take your career to the next level.

THE SKY'S THE LIMIT—IF YOU KNOW HOW TO PLAY THE GAME

You're not reading this book by accident. You're here because you want more out of your career, and you're willing to do the work to make it happen. The only question is: Are you ready to take control? Once you understand how business works, who the key players are, and how to align yourself with their goals, there is no limit to what you can achieve.

By the time you turn the last page, you'll have a roadmap to not just climb the corporate ladder, but to build a career that grows with you—one that's fueled by strategic relationships, trust, and consistent, high-impact results. It's time to stop waiting for opportunities and start *breaking boundaries*.

Part 1:

Individual Contributors

BUILDING THE FOUNDATION FOR LONG-TERM CAREER GROWTH

When you're just starting out in your career, the journey ahead can feel both exhilarating and overwhelming. The possibilities seem endless, but the path to success often feels uncertain. As an entry-level professional, your focus might be on mastering the tasks assigned to you and getting a foothold in the company. But what if you knew that this stage—the very beginning of your professional life—was the most critical in shaping your future success?

Part 1 of *Breaking Boundaries* is all about laying that foundation. It's about understanding how your work, mindset, and relationships as an individual contributor can set the stage for long-term career growth. At this level, it's not just about getting things done—it's about how you get them done. The way you approach your responsibilities now will shape the trajectory of your career. This is where you develop the habits, build the networks, and cultivate the mindset that will propel you forward.

Throughout the next three chapters, we'll follow the stories of professionals like Emma, David, and Sarah, each of whom started in entry-level positions and found ways to stand out. Emma, the marketing associate, quickly identified opportunities to improve customer satisfaction and turned her insights into actionable solutions. David, the IT support associate, understood the importance of going beyond fixing problems—he followed up with every client to ensure satisfaction, earning both trust and recognition. Sarah, starting as a project manager in IT, discovered how to navigate the complexities of mid-level roles by proactively improving team efficiency and collaboration.

In this section, we'll dive into three key aspects of excelling as an individual contributor:

1. **Chapter 1**: *Building Your Foundation* explores how entry-level professionals like Emma and David set themselves apart early in their careers by not only mastering their tasks but also looking for ways to add value and grow their influence.

2. **Chapter 2**: *Mastering Mid-Level Roles* follows Sarah's transition into a more complex, self-driven role where ownership, initiative, and strategic thinking became the keys to success.

3. **Chapter 3**: *Standing Out as a Senior-Level Contributor* focuses on James, a senior engineer, who evolved from being a technical expert into a leader and mentor, showing how to lead without formal authority and create lasting impact.

By the time you finish these chapters, you'll have a blueprint for excelling at each stage of your early career. Whether you're just entering the workforce or moving into more advanced roles, these insights will help you break through the boundaries that hold many professionals back and set you on a path toward sustained career growth.

.

Chapter 1:

Building Your Foundation – Thriving as an Entry-Level Professional

Robert begins his journey as a nervous but eager web developer, taking advice from a seasoned colleague. He decorates his modest cubicle with personal touches, signaling his first steps into the professional world.

INTRODUCTION: SETTING THE STAGE

Starting your career can feel like both an exciting adventure and an intimidating leap into the unknown. As an entry-level professional, you've just taken your first step into a new world—one where the expectations may be unclear, and the path ahead might seem more winding than straightforward. While it's tempting to think that hard work alone will carry you up the corporate ladder, the reality is more nuanced. In this stage of your career, it's not just about doing your job; it's about laying the groundwork for future success by mastering the art of creating value for your organization and positioning yourself for growth.

At this level, you are laying the foundation for everything that will follow. The habits you build, the relationships you form, and the mindset you adopt will echo throughout your career. This is the moment to establish yourself as reliable, adaptable, and capable of contributing meaningfully. You may not yet have a clear view of where you'll end up, but by taking purposeful steps now, you'll begin to shape your trajectory.

KEY EXPECTATIONS IN THIS ROLE

In an entry-level role, the expectations can often seem deceptively simple. You are tasked with learning the fundamentals of your position, becoming proficient in your assigned responsibilities, and adapting quickly to the company's processes and culture. While technical skills are critical, they are only part of the equation. What truly sets standout performers apart is their ability to go beyond the surface, demonstrating initiative, taking ownership, and contributing to the team in ways that aren't always listed in the job description.

As you navigate your role, the ability to communicate effectively becomes key. Asking the right questions, seeking clarity on expectations, and understanding how your work fits into the broader picture of the organization will show your engagement and curiosity. Being proactive in your learning and showing adaptability as you face new challenges will signal to your manager that you are ready for more. For example, consider Emma, a marketing associate who quickly mastered her daily tasks and began identifying patterns in customer feedback. She took the initiative to present her findings to her manager, offering solutions that helped the company improve customer satisfaction. By doing so, Emma not only exceeded expectations but also positioned herself as an indispensable asset to the team.

SPHERE OF INFLUENCE: WHO YOU IMPACT

At this stage in your career, your sphere of influence may feel limited, but it's more significant than you might think. You are at the beginning of developing the professional relationships that will support you throughout your journey. Your immediate circle includes your peers, direct manager, and perhaps other teams you collaborate with on projects. Each of these relationships plays a critical role in how you are perceived and how quickly you can progress.

Your peers are more than just coworkers; they are your first network. Collaborating effectively, sharing knowledge, and supporting each other creates a foundation of trust that will last as you all grow within the company. At the same time, your manager is your most important audience. They are not only evaluating your performance but also deciding when and how to advocate for your advancement. Learning to manage up—understanding what your manager needs to succeed and helping them meet their goals—can fast-track your visibility and influence.

Consider David, who was more than just an IT support associate; he was a problem-solver with a mission. Every ticket he tackled wasn't just a technical glitch to be fixed but an opportunity to create a meaningful connection. When clients reached out, often frustrated by malfunctioning systems or looming deadlines, David approached each issue with empathy, taking the time to listen—not just to the problem but to the person behind it.

Once the immediate issue was resolved, David didn't stop there. He implemented a personal touch that became his trademark: following up with every client. A day or two after resolving their issue, he would send a quick email or make a call. "How's everything working now?" he would ask, genuinely interested in their response. For David, these follow-ups weren't just a checkbox; they were an extension of his dedication to ensuring the client felt supported and valued.

This small but consistent action worked wonders. Clients who once viewed IT as a faceless, transactional department began to see David as a reliable ally. They knew that he wasn't just fixing their problems—he was ensuring they succeeded. Over time, they began requesting him by name, even thanking his manager for David's exceptional service.

CHARACTERISTICS OF HIGH PERFORMANCE IN THIS ROLE

High performance at the entry level is about more than just completing your tasks. It's about how you approach your work and your ability to recognize opportunities to add value, even in small ways. Reliability is your cornerstone. By consistently delivering on what you're tasked with and exceeding expectations when possible, you begin to establish a reputation for competence and trustworthiness.

However, reliability alone won't elevate you—you also need to show learning agility. In today's fast-paced work environments, the ability to quickly adapt to new challenges, technologies, or processes is highly valued. Those who learn quickly, ask thoughtful questions, and implement feedback are often the ones who are trusted with more responsibility. The ability to solve problems and take ownership of your tasks will also differentiate you from others at your level. Even if you don't have formal decision-making authority, you can still approach problems with a solution-oriented mindset, which will demonstrate leadership potential.

Let's take David's story a step further– David's meticulous attention to detail, coupled with his ability to turn stressful interactions into positive experiences, set him apart. He was more than just competent—he was trusted. His follow-ups not only ensured satisfaction but also uncovered recurring issues and opportunities for improvement, saving the company time and resources.

By building trust with both his clients and his manager, David became a standout performer in his role. His actions demonstrated leadership long before he carried the title, positioning him as someone others could depend on—a future leader in the making.

CHARACTERISTICS OF THE NEXT ROLE
(PREPARING FOR PROMOTION)

While you're focusing on excelling in your current position, it's never too early to think about what comes next. The transition from an entry-level role to a mid-level or specialist position requires more than just technical expertise—it demands the ability to think more strategically and take on projects that impact the larger goals of the team or company. The characteristics that will prepare you for this next level include taking initiative, expanding your awareness beyond your immediate tasks, and developing a broader understanding of the business.

Begin to look for opportunities to step outside your defined responsibilities. This could mean volunteering for a cross-departmental project, offering to help on a new initiative, or identifying inefficiencies in a process and suggesting improvements. The more you engage with the company beyond your specific duties, the more visible you'll become to leadership.

Leadership potential is often demonstrated long before someone is given a formal leadership role. It's shown through initiative, collaboration, and the ability to think critically about how your work impacts the company's broader goals. When you start to exhibit these qualities, even in small ways, you begin positioning yourself for that next promotion.

BUILDING A STRATEGY:
HOW TO CREATE BUSINESS VALUE AND INFLUENCE

Even at the entry level, you have the ability to create business value and build influence within your organization. It starts with aligning your efforts to the company's larger goals. You might feel that your role is small in the grand scheme of things, but understanding how your work contributes to the company's mission allows you to make decisions that have a bigger impact. For instance, if you work in customer service, recognize how improving customer satisfaction ties into the company's broader retention goals. This mindset shift will help you see opportunities where you can add value.

Additionally, take the time to track your accomplishments. You may not think every small success matters, but when aggregated over time, these wins demonstrate your growth and reliability. Documenting your successes will also help you when it comes time for performance reviews or promotion discussions.

Building influence starts with building relationships. Be proactive in seeking out mentors, forming connections with peers in other departments, and learning about different areas of the business. These relationships will become the foundation of your network, and as you progress, the trust you've built will help open doors for new opportunities.

ROLE-SPECIFIC CHALLENGES: MOVING BEYOND TASK-ORIENTED THINKING

One of the most common challenges at the entry level is falling into the trap of focusing solely on the tasks in front of you. It's easy to get caught up in the day-to-day demands of your role and miss the bigger picture. However, if you want to stand out and position yourself for advancement, you need to develop the habit of thinking strategically, even from the start.

The transition from a task-oriented mindset to a strategic one begins by asking yourself questions about how your work fits into the larger goals of the company. For example, how does completing this report help my manager make better decisions? Or how can my role in this project improve team performance? By thinking in terms of outcomes and impact, you'll start to develop the strategic thinking that's necessary for higher-level roles.

COMMON PITFALLS TO AVOID

While it's important to focus on excelling in your role, there are a few common pitfalls that can derail your progress. One of the biggest is failing to seek feedback. At this stage, feedback is your most valuable tool for growth. Don't wait for your manager to offer it—ask for it. By showing that you're eager to improve, you demonstrate humility and a commitment to growth, both of which are highly valued.

Another pitfall is staying within your comfort zone. It's easy to stick to what you know, but real growth happens when you push yourself into unfamiliar territory. Volunteer for projects that challenge you, even if you're not sure you're fully prepared. The willingness to stretch yourself shows leadership that you're ready for more responsibility.

Finally, don't overlook the importance of building relationships. It's tempting to think that networking is something that only happens at higher levels, but the truth is that the relationships you build now will be the foundation of your future network. Take the time to connect with your colleagues, learn from them, and offer your help when needed.

WORDS OF WISDOM

Don't mistake effort for results. In early stages, it's easy to believe that hard work alone will lead to promotion. However, promotion comes from visible impact, not just hours clocked in. Focus on learning how to demonstrate the business value you bring. Are you actively seeking feedback? Are you aligning your work with company goals, not just completing tasks? Self-reflection: Are you working hard on things that matter or just working hard?

CONCLUSION: PREPARING FOR THE NEXT LEVEL

Your success at the entry level is about more than just doing the work—it's about developing the skills, relationships, and mindset that will carry you forward. By taking ownership of your role, thinking strategically about how you can contribute, and consistently looking for ways to grow, you're setting the stage for the next phase of your career. In the next chapter, we'll explore how to transition from executing tasks to managing more complex responsibilities and building a long-term career path that aligns with your goals.

Chapter 2:

Mastering Mid-Level Roles – Taking Ownership of Your Growth

Now more confident, Robert takes charge of a team meeting, jotting ideas on a whiteboard. His focused leadership earns him the trust of his peers, marking his growth into a proactive contributor.

INTRODUCTION: SETTING THE STAGE

As you move into mid-level roles, the game begins to change. No longer are you just responsible for completing tasks—now, you're expected to think critically about the work itself, how it fits into the company's strategy, and how you can elevate your contributions. At this stage, you are becoming less of a task-taker and more of a problem solver, someone who can be trusted to identify challenges, provide solutions, and execute without constant supervision.

Moving into mid-level positions marks a critical juncture in your career where ownership of your own growth becomes essential. The opportunities for development are now more self-driven. The best mid-level professionals don't wait for instructions—they anticipate needs, think beyond their immediate responsibilities, and start shaping their career path proactively.

KEY EXPECTATIONS IN THIS ROLE

At the mid-level, you are no longer a passive participant in the work environment. You're expected to take greater ownership of your tasks, manage your time efficiently, and start contributing to the team on a broader scale. You'll be balancing a more complex workload while learning to navigate cross-functional teams and growing your influence within the organization.

When Sarah stepped into her role as a project manager, she initially focused on the basics: managing schedules, tracking deliverables, and ensuring her team stayed on target. However, as she became immersed in more complex projects, she began noticing a recurring issue—miscommunication during critical handoffs was causing delays and creating frustration. Instead of treating these challenges as inevitable, Sarah approached them as opportunities for improvement. She carefully mapped out the workflow, identifying inefficiencies and gaps, and proposed a streamlined approach using a project management tool that could centralize communication and improve accountability. When pitching her solution to leadership, she didn't just present the tool—she shared a detailed plan, complete with expected outcomes and benefits. Her initiative not only increased productivity but also energized her team, who appreciated her forward-thinking approach to reducing their workload and frustrations.

As Sarah's responsibilities grew, so did the complexity of her role. She found herself managing multiple cross-functional projects, requiring constant communication with stakeholders from departments such as marketing and operations. Understanding that successful collaboration relied on trust and rapport, Sarah proactively scheduled meetings to better understand each department's unique challenges. For example, when marketing faced delays due to incomplete data from IT, Sarah stepped in to bridge the gap, coordinating an expedited timeline that allowed the campaign to launch on schedule. These efforts highlighted her ability to align different teams' objectives while managing her own growing workload. Sarah's combination of strategic thinking, clear communication, and genuine interest in helping others established her as a problem-solver who could navigate complexity and deliver results.

SPHERE OF INFLUENCE: WHO YOU IMPACT

Your influence at the mid-level expands beyond your immediate team. You are now interacting with colleagues across departments, collaborating on projects that require cross-functional expertise, and sometimes managing smaller teams or mentoring entry-level employees. Your ability to work well with others, communicate effectively, and deliver results will determine how much influence you gain.

Consider how Sarah expanded her influence beyond her immediate team. Realizing that the success of her projects depended on input from multiple departments, Sarah built connections with key stakeholders across the organization. She took the time to understand how each team's priorities intersected with her own, fostering partnerships that made collaboration more seamless. For instance, Sarah's knack for asking the right questions and offering insightful suggestions turned her into a sought-after resource during cross-departmental initiatives. Her growing reputation for competence and reliability meant that colleagues began seeking her input on projects outside of her scope, further elevating her role within the company..

CHARACTERISTICS OF HIGH PERFORMANCE IN THIS ROLE

Success at the mid-level hinges on your ability to balance both execution and strategic thinking. High performers in these roles are not only reliable in completing their work but also proactive in anticipating problems before they arise. They take ownership of their responsibilities and are always looking for ways to improve processes or outcomes.

High performers like Sarah demonstrate a mix of execution and strategic foresight. She didn't just aim to check tasks off her list—she actively sought ways to refine workflows, simplify processes, and reduce redundancies. Sarah's work wasn't just about meeting deadlines; it was about positioning her team for long-term success. By consistently aligning her projects with the company's larger goals, Sarah ensured that her contributions not only benefited her department but also had a broader organizational impact.

CHARACTERISTICS OF THE NEXT ROLE
(PREPARING FOR PROMOTION)

To move from a mid-level position to a senior individual contributor or management role, the key shift is in your ability to take on more responsibility and start leading initiatives, either formally or informally.

The next role requires you to manage complexity, think beyond immediate goals, and start focusing on long-term strategies.

Sarah's readiness for promotion became evident as she took on larger, more complex responsibilities and started mentoring junior team members. For example, she coached a new hire on navigating cross-functional projects, equipping them with tools and strategies to succeed. Meanwhile, Sarah began volunteering for high-stakes initiatives, such as implementing a new system to improve company-wide resource allocation. These actions showed she wasn't waiting for a formal leadership title—she was already leading by improving processes, guiding others, and aligning her team's goals with the company's strategic priorities.

BUILDING A STRATEGY:
HOW TO CREATE BUSINESS VALUE AND INFLUENCE

Creating business value at the mid-level is about learning to operate in a more strategic capacity. Start by understanding how your team's goals align with the company's broader objectives. Whether it's through improving efficiencies, reducing costs, or driving innovation, the more you can demonstrate tangible contributions to the organization's success, the more valuable you become.

Sarah's ability to create business value became apparent when she addressed her team's inefficiencies in delivering projects. Instead of simply pointing out the problem, she took it upon herself to research solutions, identifying a project management tool that improved productivity by 20%. By presenting her findings with a focus on tangible benefits and guiding her team through its implementation, Sarah not only solved a recurring issue but also positioned herself as someone capable of thinking strategically and delivering measurable results.

ROLE-SPECIFIC CHALLENGES: TRANSITIONING FROM EXECUTION TO STRATEGY

The biggest challenge at this stage is moving beyond a purely execution-focused mindset and beginning to think more strategically. It's easy to get caught up in the day-to-day tasks and lose sight of the bigger picture, but to grow into a senior role, you need to show that you can anticipate problems, plan for the future, and align your work with the organization's long-term goals.

For Sarah, the pivotal moment came when she stopped viewing her responsibilities as isolated tasks and started connecting them to the company's broader success. This shift in mindset allowed her to focus on long-term strategies, like ensuring cross-departmental alignment, mentoring her team, and introducing tools that enhanced productivity company-wide. By balancing her workload while thinking strategically, Sarah exemplified the qualities of a leader ready to move into a senior role.

COMMON PITFALLS TO AVOID

One of the most common mistakes at this stage is failing to delegate or share responsibility. Mid-level professionals often feel the pressure to prove themselves by doing everything on their own. However, real growth comes when you learn to leverage the strengths of others. Don't fall into the trap of micromanaging or overextending yourself—learn to trust your team, collaborate effectively, and delegate when appropriate.

WORDS OF WISDOM

Stop waiting for someone to manage your growth. Mid-level professionals often plateau when they rely on managers to offer growth opportunities. Start taking ownership by seeking mentorship, learning new skills, and stepping into leadership informally. Waiting to be invited to the next level is a trap—initiative breaks through. Self-reflection: Are you waiting for permission to grow, or are you actively creating your own opportunities?

CONCLUSION: PREPARING FOR THE NEXT LEVEL

As you continue to grow in your mid-level role, the key to advancing is taking ownership, thinking strategically, and expanding your influence within the company. The skills you develop here will be critical as you move into more senior roles, where you'll be expected to not only manage complexity but also lead others through it. In the next chapter, we'll explore the journey of senior individual contributors and how to lead without a formal title.

Chapter 3:

Standing Out as a Senior-Level Contributor – Leading Without a Title

Robert presents to a room of managers and peers, commanding attention with his insights. Though he lacks an official title, his actions and ideas position him as an informal leader.

INTRODUCTION: SETTING THE STAGE

Reaching the senior level as an individual contributor marks a pivotal moment in your career. At this stage, you've likely become a subject-matter expert or a go-to person in your department, and your contributions are critical to the success of the team or company. However, the next step in your career requires more than technical expertise. It's about learning how to lead, influence, and drive change—even without a formal title.

As a senior-level contributor, you have the opportunity to shape decisions, influence others, and guide projects from a place of deep expertise. Your challenge now is to leverage that expertise to lead and inspire, while preparing yourself for the next step into formal leadership or management roles.

KEY EXPECTATIONS IN THIS ROLE

At the senior individual contributor level, your work is less about day-to-day execution and more about driving larger initiatives, solving complex problems, and mentoring others. You're expected to provide thought leadership in your area of expertise and collaborate across departments to deliver strategic outcomes.

For James, the shift from solving technical problems to driving larger initiatives marked a turning point in his career. Known for his unmatched ability to tackle complex coding issues, James realized that technical expertise alone wouldn't take him to the next level. He began investing his time in mentoring junior engineers, showing them how to approach challenging problems and guiding them toward success. Beyond mentoring, James proactively sought out leadership opportunities by volunteering to lead critical projects, coordinating with multiple teams to ensure alignment between technical execution and business objectives. His actions demonstrated that he was more than an expert—he was a leader in practice, earning the respect of colleagues and senior management alike.

As he became more involved in strategic discussions, James started identifying recurring pain points in the development process that slowed delivery timelines. Rather than treating these inefficiencies as isolated issues, he analyzed their root causes and proposed process improvements that saved the company significant time and resources. By combining his technical acumen with a broader organizational perspective, James elevated his contributions from solving individual problems to shaping solutions that drove company-wide value.

SPHERE OF INFLUENCE: WHO YOU IMPACT

At this stage, your influence extends beyond your immediate team. You're working with cross-functional teams, engaging with senior leadership, and possibly interacting with clients or external stakeholders. Your ability to communicate effectively and influence others without formal authority is critical to your success.

James's role required him to interact with a variety of stakeholders, from product managers to UX designers to marketing leads. Initially, these cross-functional collaborations felt daunting, as each group had unique goals and priorities. But James quickly recognized that understanding these perspectives was key to success. He made an effort to engage with stakeholders in one-on-one settings, asking questions to uncover their challenges and offering insights on how technical solutions could address their needs.

For example, when a product launch was delayed due to misaligned priorities between the development and marketing teams, James stepped in to bridge the gap. He facilitated conversations that clarified expectations and realigned timelines, ensuring a successful launch. By consistently acting as a connector and problem-solver, James built trust with colleagues across departments, extending his influence far beyond his official role and solidifying his reputation as someone who could deliver results through collaboration.

CHARACTERISTICS OF HIGH PERFORMANCE IN THIS ROLE

High-performing senior individual contributors are not just experts in their field—they are also leaders in practice, even if they don't hold formal leadership titles. They guide projects, mentor peers, and contribute to the company's long-term strategy by leveraging their expertise.

James didn't just excel at his core responsibilities—he raised the bar for what it meant to be a senior-level contributor. By working closely with cross-functional teams, he gained insights into how technical decisions impacted broader business goals. His strategic input became invaluable during product roadmap discussions, where he advocated for scalable, future-proof solutions that balanced immediate needs with long-term vision.

Mentoring junior staff was another area where James shined. He created opportunities for less experienced engineers to take on meaningful projects under his guidance, empowering them while lightening his own workload. By fostering a culture of growth and collaboration, James not only helped elevate his team but also demonstrated leadership in action.

CHARACTERISTICS OF THE NEXT ROLE
(PREPARING FOR PROMOTION)

The transition from senior individual contributor to a formal leadership or management role requires a shift in mindset. While your technical expertise remains valuable, your focus must shift to leading people, managing teams, and driving organizational success. In the next role, you'll be responsible for setting direction, managing performance, and making decisions that affect not only your team but also the company's strategic objectives.

James understood that transitioning into a formal leadership role would require more than technical expertise. He began actively developing his leadership skills by leading internal workshops, where he shared his knowledge on advanced development techniques and best practices. These workshops not only enhanced team capabilities but also showcased his ability to inspire and guide others.

Additionally, James took ownership of end-to-end project delivery for high-stakes initiatives. By managing timelines, aligning stakeholders, and ensuring successful execution, he demonstrated his readiness to handle the complexities of management. By the time the opportunity for promotion arose, James had already proven he could balance technical excellence with people leadership, making him the clear choice for a managerial position.

BUILDING A STRATEGY:
HOW TO CREATE BUSINESS VALUE AND INFLUENCE

As a senior-level contributor, your strategy should focus on driving innovation and creating long-term value for the company. Whether it's by leading high-visibility projects, mentoring others, or contributing to cross-functional initiatives, you can create significant business value by aligning your efforts with the company's broader goals.

James's ability to create business value was rooted in his knack for aligning technical solutions with organizational goals. For instance, he spearheaded an initiative to automate key parts of the development process, reducing the time spent on repetitive tasks by 30%. This not only improved team efficiency but also allowed engineers to focus on higher-value work, driving innovation.

James also recognized the importance of nurturing talent within his team. By mentoring junior engineers and creating pathways for their growth, he ensured that the company had a strong pipeline of future leaders. These efforts didn't just benefit the individuals he mentored—they positioned James as someone deeply invested in the organization's long-term success.

ROLE-SPECIFIC CHALLENGES: LEADING WITHOUT FORMAL AUTHORITY

One of the most significant challenges at this level is learning how to lead without formal authority. You may not yet have a management title, but you are expected to guide projects, mentor peers, and influence decisions. The key to overcoming this challenge is building trust and demonstrating your value through collaboration, expertise, and communication.

James' challenge now was influencing without formal authority. To succeed, he focused on building trust with his peers and stakeholders by consistently delivering high-quality work and fostering open communication. Rather than imposing his ideas, James used his expertise to guide discussions and offer solutions that aligned with everyone's objectives.

When the company faced a particularly contentious decision about whether to overhaul a core platform, James stepped up. He gathered data, facilitated discussions between teams with differing opinions, and presented a balanced recommendation to leadership. His ability to navigate this complex situation and unite diverse perspectives was a testament to his leadership capabilities, even in the absence of an official title.

COMMON PITFALLS TO AVOID

A common mistake at this stage is becoming too focused on technical expertise and neglecting leadership development. While it's essential to maintain your subject-matter expertise, failing to develop your leadership skills can limit your ability to progress into management roles.

James realized that while his technical skills were valuable, his long-term success depended on his ability to lead and inspire others. By focusing on both technical expertise and leadership development, he positioned himself for continued growth.

WORDS OF WISDOM

Stop defining leadership by title. Many get stuck because they believe that true leadership comes only with a title. Real leaders influence regardless of their role. Start solving problems beyond your immediate responsibilities, and people will naturally start seeing you as a leader. Self-reflection: Are you waiting for a title to lead, or are you already demonstrating leadership qualities in your current position?

CONCLUSION: PREPARING FOR THE NEXT LEVEL

As you continue to grow in your role as a senior individual contributor, the key to advancing is leveraging your expertise to lead and influence others. The skills you develop here will be critical as you move into formal leadership roles, where you'll be expected to manage teams and drive organizational success. In the next chapter, we'll explore the transition into managing people and how to build the foundations of effective leadership.

Part 2:

Managing People

FROM INDIVIDUAL CONTRIBUTOR TO LEADER: MASTERING THE ART OF PEOPLE MANAGEMENT

As you transition from an individual contributor to a leadership role, the rules of the game change dramatically. No longer is your success measured solely by your own output—now, you're responsible for the performance and development of others. Part 1 laid the groundwork for success by teaching you how to excel as an individual contributor, highlighting the importance of strategic thinking, ownership, and influence through the stories of Emma, David, Sarah, and James. These foundational skills become even more crucial as you step into a leadership role, where your success is intertwined with the growth and accomplishments of your team.

In Part 2, *Managing People*, we explore what it means to take the next step in your career and assume responsibility for guiding and developing others. Leadership is not simply about task delegation; it's about inspiring your team, fostering trust, and aligning their work with the broader goals of the company. This shift requires a new mindset and skillset—one that builds on the foundation of Part 1 but extends into more complex, people-centric challenges.

Take Karen's journey as an example. Like you, she started out as an individual contributor—an accomplished marketing associate who knew her role inside and out. But when Karen was promoted to team lead, she quickly learned that leadership was about more than her technical expertise. She had to learn how to motivate her team, manage their performance, and communicate effectively with senior leadership. Karen's transition highlights the pivotal moment when personal performance must evolve into team performance, and how this transition requires a deeper understanding of both people and strategy.

In Part 2, we'll explore three key aspects of people management:

1. **Chapter 4**: *Stepping into Leadership* follows Karen as she moves into her first leadership role, showing how to balance personal performance with the responsibility of guiding a team and aligning their work with organizational goals.

2. **Chapter 5**: *Stepping into Management* focuses on Maria, a newly promoted manager, as she navigates the complexities of managing a larger group, balancing short-term results with long-term team development, and driving organizational impact.

3. **Chapter 6**: *Managing Managers* tells the story of Raj, who not only leads his own team but also guides other team leads, demonstrating how to scale leadership and build influence across an organization.

The transition from individual contributor to leader is one of the most critical—and often most challenging—steps in your career. By the time you finish these chapters, you'll have a clear understanding of how to manage people effectively, foster a culture of accountability, and create lasting business value through the collective efforts of your team. Whether you're stepping into a leadership role for the first time or looking to refine your management skills, Part 2 will provide you with the tools and insights you need to succeed.

Chapter 4:

Stepping into Leadership – Becoming a Supervisor or Team Lead

Sitting at the head of a small table, Robert delegates tasks with balance and empathy. His approachable leadership style encourages his team to ask questions and collaborate effectively.

INTRODUCTION: SETTING THE STAGE

Transitioning into your first leadership role is both exciting and challenging. As a supervisor or team lead, you're no longer just responsible for your own work—you're now accountable for the performance and success of others. This shift from individual contributor to leader requires a new set of skills, including managing people, delegating tasks, and fostering a team culture that drives success.

Stepping into leadership for the first time is a pivotal moment. It marks the point where your responsibilities expand beyond just delivering results; now, you're shaping the success of your team. How you navigate this transition will define the foundations of your leadership journey. You'll need to learn to balance being a peer and a leader, guiding your team while also managing your own workload.

KEY EXPECTATIONS IN THIS ROLE

As a supervisor or team lead, you're expected to guide, support, and motivate your team. You'll likely still have your own responsibilities to manage, but a significant part of your role now is ensuring that your team delivers on its goals. This means learning to delegate effectively, monitor performance, and provide feedback. You'll also need to manage relationships, not just with your team but with senior leadership, ensuring alignment between the team's efforts and the broader organizational objectives.

When Karen transitioned from senior marketing associate to team lead, she quickly realized that leadership required an entirely new approach. As a high-performing individual contributor, Karen had thrived by focusing on her own output, but now, her success depended on the performance of her entire team. Initially, she struggled with the temptation to step in and take over tasks herself, especially when deadlines loomed. However, she soon recognized that true leadership meant empowering her team to take ownership of their work. Karen began delegating more effectively, assigning tasks based on each team member's strengths and providing clear guidance to ensure success.

To build trust and foster a sense of accountability, Karen prioritized open communication with her team. She held regular one-on-one meetings to discuss progress, address challenges, and provide constructive feedback. Her ability to balance support with high expectations created a culture where her team felt both challenged and valued. Over time, this approach improved not only individual performance but also the group's overall cohesion and effectiveness, allowing Karen to focus more on driving strategic initiatives rather than managing day-to-day tasks.

SPHERE OF INFLUENCE: WHO YOU IMPACT

As a team lead, your sphere of influence expands significantly. You are now responsible for the performance and development of your team, which means your actions directly impact their success. You'll also work closely with senior management to ensure that your team's efforts align with the company's overall strategy.

As a team lead, Karen's influence naturally extended beyond her immediate team. Recognizing that her team's success relied on effective collaboration with other departments, she made it a priority to build relationships across the organization. For example, when a product launch required input from both marketing and sales, Karen proactively reached out to the sales team to align their efforts. By fostering these cross-functional relationships, Karen ensured that her team's work was integrated seamlessly into broader company initiatives.

Karen also advocated for her team at the leadership level, using performance metrics to highlight their contributions and secure additional resources. Her ability to articulate how her team's efforts supported company goals earned her the trust of senior management. By positioning herself as a bridge between her team and upper leadership, Karen enhanced her sphere of influence and demonstrated her readiness for greater responsibility.

At this level, your relationships with your team members are crucial. You must earn their trust by being transparent, approachable, and consistent. You're also responsible for fostering a positive team culture where collaboration, communication, and accountability thrive.

CHARACTERISTICS OF HIGH PERFORMANCE IN THIS ROLE

High-performing supervisors and team leads excel in three key areas: communication, delegation, and team development. First, communication is essential—your team looks to you for direction, feedback, and support, so clear, consistent communication is crucial. Secondly, delegation is a critical skill that many new leaders struggle with. It's important to trust your team to handle tasks and avoid the temptation to do everything yourself. Lastly, team development becomes one of your top priorities. A good leader isn't just focused on achieving short-term results—they are committed to helping their team members grow.

Karen's success as a team lead stemmed from her focus on three key areas: communication, delegation, and development. She honed her communication skills by ensuring that her team always understood their goals and the context behind them. When implementing a new marketing strategy, for instance, Karen took the time to explain how the team's work aligned with the company's overall vision, which inspired her team to approach their tasks with renewed purpose.

In terms of delegation, Karen moved beyond simply assigning tasks—she empowered her team members to make decisions and take ownership of their work. By encouraging them to stretch their skills and providing constructive feedback, she created a culture of growth. Her commitment to team development was evident in her tailored approach, identifying individual strengths and helping each team member reach their potential. This investment not only boosted performance but also fostered loyalty and trust within her team.

CHARACTERISTICS OF THE NEXT ROLE
(PREPARING FOR PROMOTION)

As a team lead, you are laying the groundwork for moving into more senior management roles, such as manager or senior manager. To advance, you'll need to demonstrate that you can manage both the performance of your team and the strategic goals of the company. Your ability to align your team's work with broader organizational objectives will be a key factor in your promotion.

Karen understood that to move into a management role, she needed to show that her leadership was driving tangible business results. By tracking her team's performance, presenting data on improvements, and aligning her team's work with company-wide initiatives, she positioned herself as a key contributor to the company's success.

BUILDING A STRATEGY:
HOW TO CREATE BUSINESS VALUE AND INFLUENCE

In your role as a team lead, your focus should shift to how you can create value not just through your own work but through the collective output of your team. This involves setting clear goals, ensuring alignment with company objectives, and regularly communicating the team's successes to upper management. Building a strategy means being proactive in identifying opportunities for your team to contribute to the company's larger goals, whether through improving processes, delivering key projects, or enhancing productivity.

Karen knew that her role as a team lead wasn't just about delivering short-term results; it was about positioning her team to create long-term value for the company. One of her most significant contributions came when she analyzed her team's workflow and identified inefficiencies that were slowing down project delivery. By streamlining processes and implementing new collaboration tools, Karen increased her team's productivity by 15%.

She didn't stop there. Karen ensured that leadership was aware of these improvements by presenting data that demonstrated the team's impact on broader business goals. Her ability to connect her team's achievements to the company's success not only highlighted her leadership capabilities but also reinforced the value of her team's work, securing their reputation as a high-performing group.

ROLE-SPECIFIC CHALLENGES:
BALANCING LEADERSHIP AND PEER RELATIONSHIPS

One of the most common challenges for new supervisors is managing the shift from being a peer to being a leader. It can be difficult to balance the need to maintain positive relationships with former peers while also holding them accountable for their work. This requires a new level of emotional intelligence—understanding how to motivate and manage others without damaging relationships.

Managing the shift from peer to leader was one of Karen's challenges. Many of her team members were former colleagues, and maintaining positive relationships while holding them accountable for their performance required careful navigation. Karen addressed this by being transparent about her new responsibilities and setting clear expectations from the outset.

By focusing on fairness and open communication, Karen was able to earn her team's respect without alienating her former peers. She cultivated an environment where feedback flowed both ways, ensuring that her team felt heard while maintaining her authority as their leader. This balance between camaraderie and professionalism became a cornerstone of her leadership style.

COMMON PITFALLS TO AVOID

A common pitfall for new supervisors is trying to do everything themselves. It can be tempting to step in and take over when things aren't going smoothly, but this often leads to burnout and doesn't help your team develop the skills they need. Learning to delegate effectively is one of the most important skills you'll need to succeed in this role.

Another mistake is failing to provide timely and constructive feedback. As a leader, it's your responsibility to guide your team and help them grow, and that requires regular, honest communication about performance.

WORDS OF WISDOM

Don't fall into the trap of doing, rather than leading. New leaders often struggle because they continue to do the work instead of empowering their team to take ownership. Break the habit of micromanaging by delegating effectively and building trust. Remember, you're no longer judged solely on your own output, but on the success of the entire team. Self-reflection: Are you holding on to tasks that your team could handle, or are you empowering them to succeed?

CONCLUSION: PREPARING FOR THE NEXT LEVEL

Success as a team lead comes from your ability to guide and support your team while aligning their work with the company's goals. By developing your leadership skills, building strong relationships, and delivering results through your team, you'll be ready to take the next step into a management role. In the next chapter, we'll explore what it means to move into management and how to lead larger teams while balancing strategic objectives.

Chapter 5:

Stepping Into Management – Leading with Accountability and Growth

Robert, now a manager, stands before his team reviewing key metrics and fostering a growth-oriented discussion. His blend of seriousness and support creates a culture of accountability.

INTRODUCTION: SETTING THE STAGE

Becoming a manager is a significant step in your leadership journey. It's the point where you transition from being a team lead, responsible for guiding a small group, to managing an entire team, department, or function. As a manager, the focus expands: your responsibilities are now more complex, your influence grows, and you are accountable for not just your team's performance, but also its development.

Stepping into this role requires mastering the art of balancing the team's immediate needs with long-term growth, fostering a high-performance culture while aligning your team's objectives with the company's larger goals. This is where you begin to refine the skills that will one day prepare you to manage other managers—accountability, delegation, team development, and strategic decision-making.

KEY EXPECTATIONS IN THIS ROLE

As a manager, your role becomes multifaceted. You are expected to deliver results through your team, ensure each individual is performing to their potential, and cultivate a culture of accountability and growth. You're also responsible for aligning your team's goals with the larger organizational objectives, ensuring that every person you lead understands how their contributions affect the broader company mission.

Maria's transition from team lead to managing an entire customer success department was both exciting and daunting. Previously, her focus had been on guiding a small, cohesive team through their daily tasks. Now, her responsibilities required her to oversee multiple individuals with diverse skills, personalities, and career goals. Initially, Maria found herself gravitating toward the familiar—focusing on short-term performance metrics and stepping in to fix problems herself. However, she quickly realized that as a manager, her success would hinge on her ability to enable others to excel rather than trying to do it all herself.

To navigate this transition, Maria prioritized clear communication and accountability. She held team-wide meetings to set expectations and regularly checked in with each team member to understand their challenges and aspirations. By fostering this open dialogue, Maria ensured that her team felt supported while staying aligned with the department's objectives. At the same time, she began to shift her mindset from task management to team development, focusing on how to grow her team's skills and capabilities for the future.

SPHERE OF INFLUENCE: WHO YOU IMPACT

In a management role, your sphere of influence widens significantly. You are no longer leading a single team but managing several individuals or multiple small teams, depending on the size of your department. You also begin to collaborate more closely with senior management, ensuring that your team's performance aligns with the company's overall strategic direction.

Maria's influence grew significantly as she stepped into her management role. She understood that her team didn't operate in isolation and began attending cross-departmental meetings to build stronger relationships with other managers. By collaborating with leaders from sales, marketing, and product development, Maria gained insights into how her team's work impacted the company's broader goals. For instance, she discovered that delays in customer onboarding were affecting the sales team's ability to close deals. Maria worked with both teams to streamline the onboarding process, significantly reducing delays and improving customer satisfaction.

Maria also became an advocate for her team at the senior management level. She took the initiative to regularly report on her team's achievements and challenges, ensuring they received the resources and recognition they needed to succeed. This dual focus on collaboration and advocacy positioned Maria as a key player not just within her department but across the organization.

CHARACTERISTICS OF HIGH PERFORMANCE IN THIS ROLE

High-performing managers excel at fostering accountability and team development while driving results. They understand that their success is measured not just by what they accomplish individually but by the performance and growth of their team. To perform well as a manager, you need to balance immediate operational needs with a longer-term focus on developing your people.

Maria's approach to leadership emphasized fostering accountability and development within her team. She implemented measurable performance goals and provided her team with regular, actionable feedback to help them stay on track. By clearly communicating how their efforts aligned with the company's mission, Maria inspired her team to take ownership of their roles and perform at their best.

One of Maria's standout achievements was her commitment to team development. She identified high-potential team members and provided them with opportunities to stretch their skills, such as leading customer workshops or taking ownership of key accounts. By investing in their growth, Maria not only enhanced her team's capabilities but also built a sense of loyalty and motivation that contributed to their long-term success.

CHARACTERISTICS OF THE NEXT ROLE (PREPARING FOR PROMOTION)

To move from managing a team to managing managers, you must demonstrate mastery of leadership fundamentals—accountability, delegation, and development—while also showing that you can think strategically and operate at a higher level of complexity. The next step will require you to manage multiple leaders, each of whom will have their own teams, so developing your ability to lead through others is critical.

Maria recognized that to prepare for the next stage of her career, she needed to further develop her leadership skills, especially in delegation and strategic decision-making. She began mentoring more junior managers, helping them develop their teams while still holding them accountable for their results. This shift in focus—from managing individuals to guiding other leaders—helped Maria prepare for the more complex challenges of senior management.

BUILDING A STRATEGY:
HOW TO CREATE BUSINESS VALUE AND INFLUENCE

At this stage, building a strategy involves aligning your team's efforts with the organization's larger goals while ensuring that each team member is contributing at their highest level. This requires a focus on both results and people development—ensuring that your team is delivering on immediate objectives while also growing in their capabilities for the future.

As a manager, Maria's focus shifted to creating value through her team's collective output. One of her first initiatives was streamlining workflows to improve efficiency. By implementing a more structured approach to customer issue resolution, Maria's team reduced response times by 20%, which led to higher customer satisfaction scores and a noticeable impact on the company's bottom line.

Maria also made a point to communicate these results to senior leadership. She presented detailed reports on her team's performance, showcasing how their improvements aligned with the company's broader goals. Her ability to quantify the team's contributions not only enhanced her credibility as a leader but also strengthened her team's reputation within the organization.

ROLE-SPECIFIC CHALLENGES:
BALANCING IMMEDIATE RESULTS WITH LONG-TERM GROWTH

One of the most significant challenges new managers face is balancing the need to deliver immediate results with the responsibility of developing their team for long-term success. It's easy to get caught up in the day-to-day demands of managing a team, but to grow into a higher leadership role, you must focus on building a team that can succeed without your constant involvement.

Initially, Maria struggled to balance the demands of delivering immediate results with the need to develop her team for the future. She often found herself stepping in to resolve customer issues personally, leaving little time for strategic planning or team development. Recognizing this pattern, Maria made a deliberate effort to delegate more responsibilities to her team.

For example, she empowered one of her senior associates to lead the rollout of a new customer onboarding process, providing guidance when needed but allowing them to take full ownership. This shift not only freed up Maria's time for higher-level priorities but also gave her associate a chance to develop their leadership skills. Over time, Maria's focus on delegation and team development created a more self-sufficient and high-performing team, positioning her for greater strategic contributions.

COMMON PITFALLS TO AVOID

One common pitfall for new managers is micromanaging. When you transition from a team lead to a manager, it can be tempting to try to maintain control over every detail. However, this not only limits your team's ability to grow but also prevents you from focusing on the larger, more strategic aspects of your role.

Another pitfall is neglecting to provide regular feedback. As a manager, it's your responsibility to guide your team's performance and development, which means offering consistent, constructive feedback. Without this, your team may struggle to meet expectations, and individuals may feel unsupported in their growth.

WORDS OF WISDOM

Don't confuse popularity with leadership effectiveness. Many first-time managers aim to be liked, not realizing that avoiding difficult conversations can be detrimental. Accountability is key to long-term success, and it's not about being harsh, it's about being honest. Build a culture where constructive feedback is expected and appreciated. Self-reflection: Are you avoiding tough conversations for fear of being disliked, or are you holding yourself and your team accountable?

CONCLUSION: PREPARING FOR THE NEXT LEVEL

Success in a foundational management role is about delivering results through your team while also focusing on their long-term growth and development. By fostering a culture of accountability, providing ongoing feedback, and aligning your team's work with broader business objectives, you'll be well-prepared to take the next step into managing managers. In the next chapter, we'll explore the transition into this more complex role, where you'll be leading other leaders and shaping the future of your organization.

Chapter 6:

Managing Managers – Leading with Accountability and Trust

Leading other managers, Robert fosters open dialogue in a conference room, demonstrating trust and careful listening. His role emphasizes empowering others while maintaining oversight.

INTRODUCTION: SETTING THE STAGE

As you move into a management role, your responsibilities expand beyond just guiding a small team. Now, you are responsible for managing other managers or team leads, ensuring that the work they oversee aligns with the company's strategic objectives. This role requires a deeper understanding of leadership, as you'll need to inspire and manage multiple layers of accountability while fostering trust and driving results.

Being a manager is about leading people who lead others. It's no longer enough to manage the day-to-day operations—you are now responsible for the overall success of your department or function. At this stage, your focus shifts to developing other leaders, managing performance, and ensuring alignment with the organization's long-term goals.

KEY EXPECTATIONS IN THIS ROLE

As a manager, you are expected to take a more strategic approach to leadership. Your primary focus is on managing other leaders, ensuring that they are equipped to lead their teams effectively and that their work aligns with the company's broader objectives. You'll need to balance short-term performance with long-term growth, managing both the immediate needs of the business and the development of your team.

Raj's promotion to managing multiple project teams within the engineering department marked a pivotal moment in his leadership journey. Previously, his role had been focused on overseeing specific projects, ensuring that deliverables were met on time and within budget. But now, Raj's responsibilities encompassed guiding other project managers and ensuring their teams aligned with the company's strategic objectives.

Raj quickly learned that success in this expanded role required a shift in focus. Instead of being in the details of every project, he concentrated on setting clear goals for his project managers and providing them with the tools and support they needed to succeed. By fostering an environment of accountability and trust, Raj empowered his managers to lead their teams effectively while ensuring their efforts contributed to the company's broader mission.

SPHERE OF INFLUENCE: WHO YOU IMPACT

At this level, your influence extends across the organization. You are responsible for guiding other leaders, shaping their decisions, and ensuring that their teams are aligned with the company's goals. You'll also interact regularly with senior leadership, providing updates on your department's progress and contributing to strategic decision-making.

In his new role, Raj's influence extended well beyond his direct reports. He found himself regularly collaborating with department heads, cross-functional teams, and senior leadership to ensure that his teams' work aligned with broader organizational priorities. For example, when a company-wide initiative required close coordination between engineering and product development, Raj took the lead in building relationships with key stakeholders in both departments. By facilitating open communication and resolving potential conflicts early, he ensured that his project managers could focus on execution without getting bogged down in interdepartmental friction.

Raj also became an advocate for his department, frequently presenting updates to executive leadership. By clearly articulating his team's contributions and linking them to the company's strategic goals, Raj established himself as a trusted leader who could bridge the gap between operational execution and strategic vision.

CHARACTERISTICS OF HIGH PERFORMANCE IN THIS ROLE

High-performing managers excel in several key areas: strategic thinking, team development, and accountability. At this stage, you are responsible for driving the performance of your department while also ensuring that your team leads are growing as leaders. Your ability to hold others accountable while building a culture of trust is critical.

Raj's success as a manager stemmed from his ability to balance three critical areas: strategic thinking, team development, and accountability. He implemented a performance review process that tracked key metrics across all project teams, enabling him to identify trends, address inefficiencies, and celebrate successes. This data-driven approach ensured that each project manager stayed aligned with the department's goals while fostering a culture of continuous improvement.

In addition to focusing on performance, Raj prioritized the growth of his project managers. He offered regular mentoring sessions, sharing leadership techniques and decision-making frameworks that helped them grow into more effective leaders. By investing in their development, Raj not only improved his managers' performance but also built a strong pipeline of future leadership talent within his department.

CHARACTERISTICS OF THE NEXT ROLE
(PREPARING FOR PROMOTION)

The next step in your career as a manager is moving into senior management, where you'll be responsible for larger teams, broader strategic initiatives, and company-wide impact. To prepare for this transition, you'll need to demonstrate your ability to manage complex, cross-functional projects and lead teams through significant change.

Raj began preparing for his next role by taking on larger, more complex projects that required collaboration across multiple departments. He also focused on developing his leadership skills, particularly in guiding his team leads through difficult challenges and change initiatives.

BUILDING A STRATEGY:
HOW TO CREATE BUSINESS VALUE AND INFLUENCE

As a manager, your strategy should focus on driving business value through your department's performance. This means setting clear goals, aligning them with the company's objectives, and regularly measuring progress. It also involves developing your team leads, ensuring they are equipped to manage their teams effectively and drive results.

To drive value at this level, Raj concentrated on aligning his department's objectives with the company's broader strategy. One of his first initiatives involved creating a system to standardize project planning across teams. By introducing consistent methodologies and tools, he reduced project variability and improved efficiency across the board.

Raj didn't stop at operational improvements. He ensured that his team leads understood how their projects contributed to the company's long-term goals. During quarterly reviews, Raj worked with his project managers to connect individual project outcomes to broader organizational priorities, reinforcing their importance and enhancing morale. This strategic alignment not only increased the department's impact but also cemented Raj's reputation as a leader who could deliver both results and vision.

ROLE-SPECIFIC CHALLENGES:
LEADING THROUGH ACCOUNTABILITY

One of the biggest challenges at this stage is balancing accountability with trust. As a manager, you are responsible for holding your team leads accountable for their team's performance, but you also need to build trust and support them in their development. This requires a delicate balance of leadership—knowing when to step in and provide guidance, and when to trust your team leads to handle things on their own.

Raj's biggest challenge was balancing accountability with trust. When one of his project managers struggled with a high-stakes deliverable, Raj resisted the urge to take over. Instead, he provided the guidance and resources necessary for the project manager to create a recovery plan. Raj's approach sent a clear message: he trusted his managers to solve problems, but he also held them accountable for results.

This balance proved essential in building stronger relationships with his team leads. By empowering them to take ownership of their challenges while providing thoughtful support, Raj created an environment where his managers felt trusted yet motivated to perform at their best.

COMMON PITFALLS TO AVOID

One common pitfall for managers is failing to delegate effectively. At this level, your role is to guide and support your team leads, not to manage every detail of their work. Learning to trust your team leads and give them the autonomy they need to succeed is critical to your success as a manager.

Another pitfall is neglecting team development. As a manager, it's your responsibility to ensure that your team leads are growing as leaders. This means providing regular feedback, offering development opportunities, and supporting their growth.

WORDS OF WISDOM

Stop trying to be the expert in everything. As you begin managing other leaders, your role shifts from expertise in tasks to expertise in people. Break the boundary by stepping back from the day-to-day and trusting your leaders to manage their teams. Focus on developing their leadership skills and holding them accountable for results, rather than solving their problems. Self-reflection: Are you still trying to control everything, or are you developing your team's ability to lead?

CONCLUSION: PREPARING FOR THE NEXT LEVEL

Raj's ability to lead through others, align his department with strategic goals, and foster the growth of his team leads set him apart as a high-performing manager. By focusing on both short-term results and long-term development, he positioned himself for senior management, where he would take on even greater responsibilities. His journey underscores the importance of balancing trust and accountability, empowering others to lead while maintaining alignment with the company's broader mission.

Success as a manager comes from your ability to lead through others, driving results while also supporting the development of your team leads. The skills you develop here will be critical as you move into senior management, where you'll be responsible for larger teams and broader strategic initiatives. In the next chapter, we'll explore the transition into senior management and how to lead teams through complexity and change.

Chapter 7:

Senior Management – Scaling Leadership Across Teams

From a vantage point overlooking bustling teams, Robert reflects on his responsibility to ensure harmony across departments. His leadership now spans multiple teams, blending pride with measured resolve.

INTRODUCTION: SETTING THE STAGE

Transitioning into senior management marks a shift from managing a single team or department to overseeing multiple teams or functions. Your role is no longer just about meeting team objectives—it's about scaling leadership, ensuring that your teams are aligned with company-wide goals, and navigating complex challenges that require a more strategic mindset. At this level, you're guiding not only the work but the leaders under you, ensuring that the organization's vision is reflected across the board.

Senior management is about understanding the broader landscape and making decisions that affect entire departments or divisions. You're no longer just a team leader; you're a business leader, responsible for driving large-scale success through collaboration, strategic thinking, and developing leaders of leaders. This is where leadership becomes about influence, alignment, and long-term vision.

KEY EXPECTATIONS IN THIS ROLE

In senior management, the expectations rise considerably. You are now accountable for multiple teams or entire departments, and your focus shifts to broader business outcomes. You're expected to think strategically, manage resources effectively, and deliver results that align with the company's long-term objectives. Your role is to ensure that the leaders under you are aligned with these goals and that they're equipped to manage their teams effectively.

Luis's promotion to senior manager overseeing multiple manufacturing facilities required a significant shift in his leadership approach. Previously, his focus was on managing the operations of a single facility, ensuring efficiency and meeting production goals. Now, his role demanded a broader perspective, balancing the performance of multiple facilities while aligning their efforts with the company's strategic objectives.

Luis quickly realized that his success would depend on his ability to scale leadership—guiding plant managers to take ownership of their operations while fostering alignment across teams.

To meet these new demands, Luis developed initiatives that addressed both immediate performance needs and long-term growth. For example, he implemented cost-reduction strategies that standardized operations across facilities, ensuring consistency while improving efficiency. At the same time, he prioritized the development of his plant managers, mentoring them on leadership practices and strategic decision-making. This dual focus on operational excellence and leadership growth allowed Luis to deliver results that impacted not just his teams but the entire organization.

SPHERE OF INFLUENCE: WHO YOU IMPACT

Your influence at the senior management level extends across the organization. You are leading other managers, collaborating with executives, and ensuring that your department's goals are integrated with the overall company strategy. You're responsible for setting the direction for multiple teams, guiding their leaders, and ensuring that each part of your organization is contributing to the broader success.

As a senior manager, Luis's influence extended well beyond his direct reports. He collaborated regularly with the executive team to understand the company's strategic goals and translate them into actionable objectives for his facilities. For instance, when the organization identified sustainability as a key priority, Luis worked with his plant managers to implement greener manufacturing practices, reducing energy usage while maintaining output.

Luis also played a pivotal role in cross-departmental collaboration, working closely with leaders in finance, marketing, and product development. By building strong relationships across the organization, he ensured that the operational strategy aligned with the company's broader goals. This horizontal influence allowed him to drive cohesion between departments, ensuring that everyone was working toward shared objectives.

At this level, you are responsible for both vertical and horizontal influence. You need to lead your own teams, but also work across departments and functions to ensure that everyone is moving in the same direction.

CHARACTERISTICS OF HIGH PERFORMANCE IN THIS ROLE

High performers in senior management excel at strategic thinking, resource management, and leadership development. They not only manage the present but also anticipate future challenges and opportunities. A senior manager who performs well is someone who can guide their department through periods of change, maintain high performance, and foster an environment where leaders and teams can thrive.

Luis demonstrated high performance by balancing strategic vision with practical execution. He proactively identified industry trends and used them to shape his department's direction. For example, he invested in advanced automation technologies, reducing manual labor costs and increasing production efficiency by 25%. This innovation not only improved short-term results but also positioned the company to stay competitive in the long term.

Beyond operational improvements, Luis focused on leadership development. He held regular workshops with his plant managers, teaching them how to handle challenges such as workforce planning and resource allocation. By empowering his leaders to think strategically, Luis cultivated a team that could adapt to change and consistently deliver strong results. This focus on development created a ripple effect of high performance across all his facilities.

At this level, your performance is measured not only by the success of your teams but by your ability to innovate and create sustainable improvements that drive business growth.

CHARACTERISTICS OF THE NEXT ROLE
(PREPARING FOR PROMOTION)

The transition from senior manager to director-level leadership requires a deeper focus on strategic vision and company-wide influence. Directors are responsible for driving large-scale change, managing cross-functional teams, and influencing decisions that affect the entire organization. To prepare for this role, you must demonstrate your ability to lead through complexity, manage large-scale initiatives, and think beyond the scope of your immediate department.

Luis began preparing for his transition to director by taking on cross-functional projects, collaborating with other departments, and aligning his teams with the company's long-term strategic goals. He developed a deeper understanding of how each function within the company worked together, which positioned him as a candidate for director-level responsibilities.

BUILDING A STRATEGY:
HOW TO CREATE BUSINESS VALUE AND INFLUENCE

As a senior manager, your strategy should focus on maximizing the value your teams bring to the organization. This includes optimizing performance, identifying opportunities for innovation, and ensuring that your department is aligned with the company's strategic objectives. Additionally, you need to foster a culture of continuous improvement, where your leaders are empowered to drive change and contribute to the company's success.

Luis's strategy as a senior manager centered on maximizing value through innovation and alignment. One of his most impactful initiatives involved introducing a performance tracking system that monitored key metrics across all facilities. By analyzing this data, Luis identified opportunities for improvement and worked with his managers to implement targeted solutions.

In addition to operational excellence, Luis emphasized the importance of communication. He ensured that his plant managers understood how their individual facilities contributed to the company's overarching goals. This alignment fostered a sense of purpose and motivated teams to go above and beyond, knowing their efforts were part of a larger mission.

ROLE-SPECIFIC CHALLENGES:
NAVIGATING COMPLEXITY AND CHANGE

One of the biggest challenges at this level is navigating complexity. Senior managers are responsible for overseeing multiple teams or departments, each with their own goals, challenges, and dynamics. Managing this complexity requires a high level of coordination, communication, and flexibility. Additionally, senior managers are often responsible for leading their teams through periods of significant change, whether it's a shift in strategy, the implementation of new technology, or changes in market conditions.

Navigating complexity became a defining challenge for Luis. When his company decided to restructure its operations, consolidating two facilities into one, he had to lead his teams through the transition. The restructuring involved difficult decisions, including workforce reductions and changes to production workflows, all while maintaining morale and productivity.

Luis approached this challenge with transparency and empathy. He communicated openly with his managers and teams about the reasons behind the changes and provided resources to help them adapt. By involving his plant managers in the planning process, he empowered them to take ownership of the transition. This collaborative approach ensured a smooth integration and strengthened the trust within his teams.

COMMON PITFALLS TO AVOID

One common pitfall for senior managers is failing to delegate effectively. At this level, it's impossible to manage every detail of your teams' work, and trying to do so can lead to burnout and inefficiencies. Instead, focus on empowering your leaders to take ownership of their areas while providing the support and guidance they need to succeed.

Another pitfall is losing sight of the big picture. Senior managers are responsible for aligning their teams with the company's long-term goals, but it's easy to get caught up in the day-to-day challenges. Make sure you regularly step back to assess whether your teams are still on track to meet broader objectives.

WORDS OF WISDOM

Vision without execution is hallucination. Directors often get stuck when they focus too much on big-picture thinking but neglect the necessary steps to execute that vision. Break this boundary by aligning your strategic vision with concrete, actionable plans and ensuring your teams have the resources and direction they need. Self-reflection: Are you spending more time on vision without following through, or are you balancing vision with execution?

CONCLUSION: PREPARING FOR THE NEXT LEVEL

Luis's ability to lead through complexity, drive operational improvements, and develop other leaders positioned him as a standout senior manager. His success stemmed from his focus on aligning his teams with the company's strategic objectives while fostering innovation and continuous improvement. As he prepared for the transition to director-level leadership, Luis's experience managing multiple layers of accountability and navigating organizational change gave him the skills necessary to drive even broader impact at the company level.

Success as a senior manager comes from your ability to lead through complexity, develop other leaders, and align your teams with the company's long-term goals. As you continue to grow in this role, the next step is moving into director-level leadership, where you'll be responsible for larger-scale initiatives and broader organizational impact. In the next chapter, we'll explore what it takes to run a business as a director and how to influence decisions that shape the future of the company.

Part 3:

Running a Business

FROM LEADING TEAMS TO LEADING ORGANIZATIONS: THE ART OF RUNNING A BUSINESS

As you ascend into higher levels of leadership, the skills and lessons from Parts 1 and 2 begin to come together in a powerful way. Part 1 focused on mastering individual contribution—building the habits, relationships, and mindset that lay the foundation for a successful career. Part 2 elevated that foundation into managing people, where you learned to drive performance through others, building trust, fostering team collaboration, and aligning efforts with broader organizational goals. Now, in Part 3, we step into the most complex and strategic phase of your leadership journey: running a business.

Transitioning into business leadership means you are no longer just responsible for individual performance or team success—you're now accountable for entire functions, divisions, or departments. This is where the ability to think holistically and strategically becomes paramount. Leading at this level requires you to balance vision and execution, ensuring that your area of responsibility is not only meeting current targets but also contributing to the company's long-term success. This is where your role evolves from managing people to managing business outcomes.

Take Emily, for example. In her journey from marketing associate to director of marketing, she learned to oversee large-scale initiatives, manage budgets, and drive cross-functional collaboration. Her role no longer centered on the day-to-day tasks of marketing; instead, she was focused on how her department could strategically support the company's broader goals. Emily's success as a director came from her ability to see the big picture while executing on the finer details that made her team successful.

In this part of *Breaking Boundaries*, we'll explore how to make that leap from managing people to running the business.

1. **Chapter 8**: *Becoming a Director* follows Emily's story, highlighting how leaders must shift their focus to vision, strategy, and organizational impact at this level.

2. **Chapter 9**: *Senior Directors* continues with Amanda, a senior director of product development, as she demonstrates how to bridge strategy and execution by leading complex, cross-functional teams and managing large-scale initiatives.

3. **Chapter 10**: *Vice Presidents and Beyond* introduces Daniel, a vice president of operations, who oversees global functions, aligning business strategy with company-wide objectives and leading through uncertainty.

The transition from managing teams to leading entire business functions marks a critical turning point in your career. By the time you complete these chapters, you will understand how to lead with vision, make strategic decisions, and drive business value at the highest level. The journey from individual contributor to director requires wisdom, adaptability, and the ability to influence across the entire organization—and Part 3 will give you the roadmap to succeed.

Chapter 8:

Becoming a Director –
Leading with Vision

Robert, now a director, gazes over a city skyline while holding a strategic plan. Behind him, his team works on long-term strategies, signaling his transition to visionary leadership.

INTRODUCTION: SETTING THE STAGE

Becoming a director marks a significant transition in your leadership journey. At this level, you're responsible for overseeing entire functions or divisions of the company, managing complex initiatives, and driving long-term success. Directors are strategic leaders, tasked with turning the company's vision into actionable plans and ensuring that every part of the business they oversee contributes to the broader organizational goals.

As a director, you're no longer managing just people—you're managing the success of the business. Your role is to provide leadership at a high level, make decisions that impact the future of the company, and guide your teams toward achieving large-scale objectives. This is where leadership becomes about vision, strategy, and execution on a much larger scale.

KEY EXPECTATIONS IN THIS ROLE

At the director level, you are expected to think strategically, lead large-scale initiatives, and contribute to the company's long-term success. Your role is to ensure that the divisions or functions you oversee are aligned with the company's strategic objectives and are driving meaningful results. You'll need to work closely with senior leadership to shape the direction of the company, manage significant budgets and resources, and lead teams through periods of growth and change.

When Emily became director of marketing for a large tech company, her responsibilities shifted from managing teams to leading a critical business function. No longer focused solely on operational execution, Emily's role now involved crafting strategies that drove brand growth, customer acquisition, and revenue. This required her to think beyond individual campaigns and focus on how marketing efforts supported the company's long-term goals.

Emily began by developing a comprehensive marketing strategy that aligned with the company's vision. She set ambitious but achievable targets, such as increasing brand awareness by 30% and driving a 15% increase in customer acquisition within the first year. Her leadership extended to managing department heads, equipping them with the resources and support they needed to guide their teams effectively. By balancing strategic foresight with hands-on support for her leaders, Emily ensured that every level of her department was driving toward shared objectives.

SPHERE OF INFLUENCE: WHO YOU IMPACT

As a director, your influence spans the entire organization. You are responsible for leading multiple teams, managing senior leaders, and working closely with executives to shape the company's future. Your decisions have a significant impact on the success of the business, and your ability to influence others is critical to driving results.

In her position as director, Emily's impact resonated across the entire organization. She worked closely with the product, sales, and finance teams to align marketing efforts with the company's product roadmap and revenue targets. For instance, during the launch of a new flagship product, Emily collaborated with the product team to ensure that marketing campaigns highlighted the most compelling features, while also syncing timelines with the sales team's go-to-market strategy. This alignment maximized the impact of the launch, leading to a significant increase in initial sales.

Emily also became a trusted advisor to the executive team. Her ability to communicate the value of marketing initiatives in terms of business outcomes made her a key contributor to strategic discussions. Whether it was proposing investments in brand-building initiatives or presenting metrics on customer acquisition, Emily consistently demonstrated how her department's work directly supported the company's broader goals.

At this level, your influence isn't limited to your own department—you are shaping the direction of the company. Your ability to communicate effectively, build strong relationships with other leaders, and drive cross-functional collaboration is essential to your success.

CHARACTERISTICS OF HIGH PERFORMANCE IN THIS ROLE

High-performing directors are strategic thinkers who can turn vision into action. They excel at managing complexity, leading large teams, and driving results that align with the company's long-term goals. A director who performs well is someone who can navigate change, manage resources effectively, and lead their teams to achieve ambitious objectives.

Emily's success as a director was defined by her ability to balance vision with execution. She not only crafted high-level strategies but also ensured that they were implemented effectively. For example, she introduced new analytics tools that allowed her team to track the ROI of marketing campaigns in real time. This data-driven approach helped her identify which efforts were driving the most value, enabling her to reallocate resources to maximize impact.

Additionally, Emily focused on developing her department heads, ensuring they had the leadership skills needed to guide their teams through periods of growth and change. She regularly met with each leader to review performance, provide feedback, and discuss professional development opportunities. By building a strong leadership pipeline within her department, Emily created a culture of continuous improvement that extended throughout the organization.

CHARACTERISTICS OF THE NEXT ROLE
(PREPARING FOR PROMOTION)

The next step in your career as a director is moving into senior director or vice president roles, where you'll be responsible for even larger parts of the business and have a direct influence on the company's strategic direction. To prepare for this transition, you'll need to demonstrate your ability to lead through complexity, drive large-scale initiatives, and influence company-wide decisions.

Emily began preparing for her next role by taking on additional responsibilities, such as leading cross-functional projects and contributing to the company's long-term strategic planning. She also focused on building relationships with the executive team, positioning herself as a key leader within the organization.

BUILDING A STRATEGY:
HOW TO CREATE BUSINESS VALUE AND INFLUENCE

As a director, your strategy should focus on driving significant business value through the divisions or functions you oversee. This means setting ambitious goals, ensuring alignment with the company's long-term objectives, and regularly measuring progress. It also involves managing resources effectively, ensuring that your teams have the support they need to succeed while staying within budget.

Emily's strategy as a director revolved around creating both immediate and long-term value for the company. She set aggressive short-term goals for customer acquisition while also investing in brand-building initiatives designed to deliver sustained growth. For example, she launched a multi-channel branding campaign that increased awareness in new markets while driving significant engagement with existing customers.

To ensure alignment with the company's overall strategy, Emily maintained regular communication with the executive team. She provided quarterly updates on her department's progress, highlighting successes and identifying areas for improvement. This transparency not only reinforced her credibility as a leader but also ensured that her department's efforts remained tightly integrated with the company's strategic objectives.

ROLE-SPECIFIC CHALLENGES: LEADING THROUGH VISION

One of the biggest challenges directors face is leading through vision. At this level, you are responsible for setting the direction for entire functions or divisions of the company, which requires a clear understanding of the company's strategic objectives and the ability to translate that vision into actionable plans. You'll need to inspire your teams, manage significant resources, and ensure that every part of the business you oversee is contributing to the company's success.

Emily's most significant challenge came when her company decided to enter an entirely new market. This required her to craft a marketing strategy that aligned with the company's vision while also addressing the unique demands of the new audience. Emily approached this challenge by engaging her department heads in the planning process, encouraging collaboration and leveraging their insights to develop a cohesive strategy.

To inspire her teams, Emily communicated the importance of the new market to the company's long-term growth, setting clear and ambitious goals that motivated her leaders to excel. She also ensured they had the tools and resources needed to execute effectively, providing support without micromanaging. This combination of clear vision and collaborative leadership allowed her department to exceed expectations, contributing significantly to the company's success in the new market.

COMMON PITFALLS TO AVOID

One common pitfall for directors is losing sight of the long-term vision. At this level, it's easy to get caught up in the day-to-day challenges of managing multiple teams and initiatives, but it's important to regularly step back and assess whether your department is still aligned with the company's strategic goals.

Another pitfall is failing to manage resources effectively. Directors are responsible for managing significant budgets and ensuring that their teams have the resources they need to succeed. Failing to allocate resources appropriately can lead to missed opportunities and underperformance.

WORDS OF WISDOM

Avoid getting stuck in the "strategy bubble." Senior leaders can fall into the trap of staying in strategy discussions without ever moving to action. Successful leaders bring strategy to life by staying involved in how it's implemented. Ensure you're connecting high-level plans to day-to-day operations and outcomes. Self-reflection: Are you too focused on strategy at the expense of execution, or are you bridging the gap between the two?

CONCLUSION: PREPARING FOR THE NEXT LEVEL

Emily's ability to lead with vision, align cross-functional efforts, and deliver measurable results positioned her as a high-performing director. By focusing on both strategic goals and the development of her department's leaders, she created long-term value for the company while preparing for the transition to senior director or vice president roles. Her journey illustrates the importance of balancing strategy with execution, driving results while maintaining alignment with the company's broader mission.

Success as a director comes from your ability to lead with vision, manage complexity, and drive results that align with the company's long-term goals. As you continue to grow in this role, the next step is moving into senior director or vice president roles, where you'll be responsible for shaping the future of the company. In the next chapter, we'll explore what it means to lead at the executive level and how to influence decisions that shape the entire organization.

Chapter 9:

Senior Directors – Bridging Strategy and Execution

At a boardroom table, Robert connects strategy with execution, guiding junior directors with precision. His role bridges big-picture thinking and actionable results.

INTRODUCTION: SETTING THE STAGE

As you step into the role of Senior Director, the stakes are higher. You are now responsible for overseeing not only large teams but also major initiatives that impact the entire organization. At this level, your role is to bridge the gap between strategy and execution, ensuring that the company's long-term goals are realized through effective leadership and sound decision-making. Senior Directors operate at the intersection of vision and results, translating high-level strategy into actionable plans and guiding their teams to achieve measurable outcomes.

This role requires you to think holistically, managing cross-functional teams, setting strategic priorities, and making decisions that will shape the future of the company. You are not just executing on plans—you are helping to create them, ensuring that every part of the organization you oversee is aligned with the company's mission and driving business success.

KEY EXPECTATIONS IN THIS ROLE

At the Senior Director level, your expectations shift toward a greater emphasis on strategic leadership and execution. You are responsible for managing entire divisions or multiple departments, ensuring that their work aligns with the broader company strategy and contributes to long-term business goals. Your focus is no longer just on team performance, but on delivering results that affect the company's future.

Amanda's promotion to Senior Director of Product Development required her to elevate her perspective and leadership skills to an entirely new level. No longer focused on the management of a single team, she now oversaw the entire product development lifecycle across multiple teams, each with its own goals, challenges, and opportunities. Amanda's primary responsibility was to ensure that her division's work aligned with the company's long-term strategic objectives while delivering innovative products that met market demands.

To succeed in this role, Amanda shifted her focus to building and executing a comprehensive product roadmap. This involved working closely with senior leadership to set strategic priorities and translating them into actionable plans for her teams. Her ability to balance strategic thinking with operational excellence ensured that the company's innovation goals were met on time and within budget. By fostering collaboration among her department leaders, Amanda created a cohesive strategy that drove results and supported the company's vision for the future.

SPHERE OF INFLUENCE: WHO YOU IMPACT

As a Senior Director, your influence extends far beyond your direct reports. You are responsible for leading entire functions or divisions, collaborating with executive leadership, and driving cross-functional initiatives. You play a key role in shaping the company's future by ensuring that your teams are aligned with the company's strategic vision and contributing to its long-term success.

Amanda's influence as a Senior Director extended far beyond her immediate division. She regularly collaborated with marketing, sales, and finance leaders to align product development efforts with customer needs and revenue goals. For instance, during the launch of a major product line, Amanda coordinated with marketing to craft compelling messaging and with sales to refine go-to-market strategies, ensuring a seamless transition from development to customer acquisition.

At the same time, Amanda played a key role in shaping the company's overall strategy. Her ability to anticipate market trends and incorporate them into the product roadmap made her a valuable contributor to executive discussions. By presenting clear, data-driven recommendations, Amanda ensured that her division's initiatives were aligned with the company's strategic vision, further solidifying her role as a trusted leader and influencer within the organization.

At this level, your decisions impact the entire organization. You need to be able to lead through influence, manage complex relationships, and ensure that every part of your division is contributing to the company's success.

CHARACTERISTICS OF HIGH PERFORMANCE IN THIS ROLE

High-performing Senior Directors are master strategists who can turn vision into results. They excel at managing complexity, leading cross-functional teams, and driving large-scale initiatives that deliver measurable outcomes. A Senior Director who performs well is someone who can think several steps ahead, anticipating challenges and opportunities, and ensuring that their teams are aligned with the company's long-term goals.

Amanda demonstrated high performance by excelling in both strategic leadership and operational execution. Her ability to anticipate industry shifts allowed her to guide her teams toward opportunities that aligned with emerging market demands. For example, she identified a growing interest in sustainable products and led her teams to develop eco-friendly solutions, positioning the company as an innovator in the space while boosting revenue.

In addition to her strategic impact, Amanda invested heavily in developing her department leaders. She provided them with mentorship, leadership training, and resources, ensuring they had the tools to manage their teams effectively. By building a strong pipeline of capable leaders, Amanda created a ripple effect of high performance throughout her division, enabling consistent success across multiple teams.

CHARACTERISTICS OF THE NEXT ROLE
(PREPARING FOR PROMOTION)

The next step in your career as a Senior Director is moving into an executive leadership role, such as Vice President or Chief Officer. At this level, you will be responsible for shaping the overall direction of the company, influencing decisions at the highest level, and driving organizational change. To prepare for this transition, you must demonstrate your ability to lead through complexity, manage large-scale initiatives, and influence company-wide decisions.

Amanda began preparing for her transition to Vice President by taking on additional responsibilities, such as leading company-wide initiatives and contributing to the company's long-term strategic planning. She also focused on building relationships with the executive team, positioning herself as a trusted advisor and strategic leader within the organization.

BUILDING A STRATEGY:
HOW TO CREATE BUSINESS VALUE AND INFLUENCE

As a Senior Director, your strategy should focus on driving significant business value through the divisions or departments you oversee. This means setting ambitious goals, ensuring alignment with the company's long-term objectives, and regularly measuring progress. It also involves managing resources effectively, ensuring that your teams have the support they need to succeed while staying within budget.

Amanda's strategy focused on aligning her division's goals with the company's long-term vision while driving measurable outcomes. She set ambitious targets for product innovation and ensured her teams had the support and resources to achieve them. For example, Amanda implemented new tools and processes that streamlined development cycles, reducing time to market by 20%. This improvement not only boosted efficiency but also allowed the company to capitalize on market opportunities faster than competitors.

To maintain alignment with organizational objectives, Amanda established regular communication channels with the executive team. She presented quarterly progress updates, highlighting successes, addressing challenges, and demonstrating how her division's work contributed to the company's growth. This transparency reinforced her credibility and ensured that her teams remained a key driver of the company's success.

ROLE-SPECIFIC CHALLENGES:
LEADING THROUGH COMPLEXITY AND SCALE

One of the biggest challenges Senior Directors face is managing complexity and scale. At this level, you are responsible for overseeing large teams and driving initiatives that span multiple departments or functions. Managing this complexity requires a high level of coordination, communication, and strategic thinking. Additionally, Senior Directors are often responsible for leading their teams through periods of significant change, whether it's a shift in strategy, the implementation of new technology, or changes in market conditions.

One of Amanda's most significant challenges came when her company decided to enter a new market. This shift required her to navigate the complexities of developing products tailored to a new audience while maintaining the performance of existing lines. Amanda responded by engaging cross-functional teams in the planning process, ensuring alignment between product development, marketing, and sales.

Amanda also faced the challenge of managing the scale of her responsibilities. With multiple teams working on overlapping projects, she had to ensure that resources were allocated efficiently and that priorities were clear. By implementing a robust project management framework, Amanda created clarity and structure, allowing her teams to operate cohesively even in a fast-paced and demanding environment.

COMMON PITFALLS TO AVOID

One common pitfall for Senior Directors is losing sight of the long-term vision. At this level, it's easy to get caught up in the day-to-day challenges of managing large teams and initiatives, but it's important to regularly step back and assess whether your division is still aligned with the company's strategic goals.

Another pitfall is failing to manage resources effectively. Senior Directors are responsible for managing significant budgets and ensuring that their teams have the resources they need to succeed. Failing to allocate resources appropriately can lead to missed opportunities and underperformance.

WORDS OF WISDOM

The future isn't built on yesterday's successes. VPs and executives often become complacent, relying on past achievements to secure their position. Break through by continuously innovating and adapting to market changes. Focus on positioning the company to not just survive but thrive in the future. Self-reflection: Are you coasting on past wins, or are you actively positioning your team and company for future success?

CONCLUSION: PREPARING FOR THE NEXT LEVEL

Amanda's success as a Senior Director stemmed from her ability to manage complexity, align cross-functional efforts, and drive innovation that delivered measurable results. Her focus on developing leaders within her division, coupled with her ability to balance strategy and execution, positioned her as a strong candidate for executive leadership. As Amanda prepared for her next role as Vice President, she continued to refine her skills, focusing on influencing company-wide decisions and driving organizational success. Her journey exemplifies the importance of leading through vision, managing scale, and aligning every effort with the company's long-term goals.

Success as a Senior Director comes from your ability to lead through complexity, manage large-scale initiatives, and drive results that align with the company's long-term goals. As you continue to grow in this role, the next step is moving into executive leadership, where you'll be responsible for shaping the future of the company and influencing decisions at the highest level. In the final chapter, we'll explore what it takes to lead at the executive level and how to drive organizational success.

Chapter 10:

Vice Presidents and Beyond – Shaping the Future of the Business

As Vice President, Robert collaborates with C-level executives on a company roadmap. His leadership is focused on defining and shaping the organization's long-term future.

INTRODUCTION: SETTING THE STAGE

Reaching the executive level—whether as a Vice President, Senior Vice President, or Chief Officer—represents the pinnacle of your leadership journey. At this level, you are responsible for shaping the overall direction of the company, driving large-scale strategic initiatives, and ensuring the long-term success of the organization. Executives operate at the highest level of leadership, making decisions that impact every aspect of the business, from financial performance to organizational culture.

As a Vice President or beyond, your role is to provide visionary leadership, guiding the company through periods of growth, change, and innovation. You are responsible for not only leading large teams but also influencing decisions that affect the entire organization. This is where leadership becomes about creating a legacy, shaping the future of the business, and leaving a lasting impact.

KEY EXPECTATIONS IN THIS ROLE

At the executive level, the expectations are incredibly high. You are responsible for driving the overall success of the company, ensuring that every part of the organization is aligned with the company's strategic objectives and contributing to its long-term growth. Your focus is on setting the vision for the company, managing large-scale initiatives, and making decisions that will shape the future of the business.

When Daniel became Vice President of Operations for a global manufacturing company, his responsibilities expanded to a level of complexity and impact that required a shift in mindset and strategy. No longer focused solely on individual regions or teams, Daniel was now tasked with overseeing operations across multiple geographies. His mandate was to ensure alignment between operational performance and the company's long-term growth objectives.

Daniel's success stemmed from his ability to think strategically while maintaining operational excellence. He developed a company-wide operations strategy that reduced costs by 15% while improving efficiency across all regions. By focusing on optimizing processes and implementing scalable systems, Daniel ensured that his teams could meet immediate objectives while positioning the company for sustainable growth. His ability to balance short-term wins with long-term innovation defined his leadership at the executive level.

SPHERE OF INFLUENCE: WHO YOU IMPACT

As an executive, your influence extends across the entire organization. You are responsible for leading large teams, managing senior leaders, and driving decisions that impact the future of the business. You work closely with the executive team and board of directors to shape the company's strategy and ensure its long-term success.

As Vice President, Daniel's influence extended across the entire organization. His role required him to lead senior managers and their teams while collaborating with the CEO, CFO, and other executives to shape the company's overall strategy. For example, during a significant international expansion, Daniel worked closely with finance to secure the necessary resources, with marketing to understand customer needs in the new market, and with product teams to ensure operational readiness.

Daniel's ability to foster cross-functional collaboration was pivotal. He not only ensured his operations team delivered on its objectives but also helped align their work with broader business goals. His ability to influence decisions at the executive level reinforced his role as a key driver of the company's strategic success.

At this level, your influence goes beyond your own department or division— you are shaping the future of the company. Your ability to communicate effectively, build strong relationships with other executives, and drive cross-functional collaboration is essential to your success.

CHARACTERISTICS OF HIGH PERFORMANCE IN THIS ROLE

High-performing executives are visionary leaders who can turn strategy into results. They excel at managing complexity, leading large-scale initiatives, and driving long-term success for the company. An executive who performs well is someone who can inspire their teams, manage change, and make decisions that have a lasting impact on the organization.

Daniel's high performance as an executive was evident in his ability to transform strategy into tangible results. One of his standout achievements was implementing a global supply chain optimization initiative that reduced lead times by 20% and significantly improved customer satisfaction. This required not only technical expertise but also the ability to coordinate across teams, regions, and leadership levels.

In addition to operational improvements, Daniel focused on leadership development within his division. He mentored his senior leaders, equipping them with the tools and confidence to manage their teams effectively. By fostering a culture of accountability and empowerment, Daniel ensured that his leaders were prepared to navigate challenges independently, driving consistency and excellence across the organization..

BUILDING A STRATEGY:
HOW TO CREATE BUSINESS VALUE AND INFLUENCE

As an executive, your strategy should focus on driving large-scale business value through the divisions or departments you oversee. This means setting ambitious goals, ensuring alignment with the company's long-term objectives, and regularly measuring progress. It also involves managing resources effectively, ensuring that your teams have the support they need to succeed while staying within budget.

Daniel's strategy centered on maximizing value through innovation and operational efficiency. He set aggressive yet achievable targets, such as integrating advanced analytics into operations to identify inefficiencies and predict supply chain disruptions. These initiatives not only drove immediate cost savings but also positioned the company as a leader in operational innovation.

Daniel also made it a priority to communicate the impact of his division's work to the executive team and board of directors. By providing clear, data-driven insights into how his operations strategy supported the company's growth objectives, he reinforced the critical role his teams played in driving business success. This transparency built trust and strengthened his influence at the highest levels of the organization.

ROLE-SPECIFIC CHALLENGES:
LEADING THROUGH UNCERTAINTY

One of the biggest challenges executives face is leading through uncertainty. At this level, you are responsible for navigating the company through periods of significant change, whether it's a shift in strategy, market conditions, or technological advancements. Managing this uncertainty requires a high level of flexibility, strategic thinking, and resilience.

Leading through uncertainty became a defining challenge for Daniel when his company expanded into a new international market. This expansion required him to navigate unfamiliar regulatory environments, supply chain complexities, and workforce dynamics. Rather than viewing these obstacles as insurmountable, Daniel approached them with a combination of strategic planning and flexibility.

He established clear communication channels across all levels of his division, ensuring that his teams were aligned and informed. By setting realistic milestones and providing the necessary resources, Daniel guided his division through the transition while maintaining high levels of productivity and morale. His ability to lead through such complexity solidified his reputation as a resilient and adaptive leader.

COMMON PITFALLS TO AVOID

One common pitfall for executives is losing sight of the long-term vision. At this level, it's easy to get caught up in the day-to-day challenges of managing large teams and initiatives, but it's important to regularly step back and assess whether your division is still aligned with the company's strategic goals.

Another pitfall is failing to manage resources effectively. Executives are responsible for managing significant budgets and ensuring that their teams have the resources they need to succeed. Failing to allocate resources appropriately can lead to missed opportunities and underperformance.

WORDS OF WISDOM

Stop focusing only on "winning" and start focusing on leaving a legacy. At the highest level, leadership is about long-term impact, not short-term gains. Focus on creating a legacy of leadership that outlasts your tenure—by developing future leaders, fostering innovation, and driving sustainable success. Self-reflection: Are you just trying to keep the company afloat, or are you building something that will thrive long after you're gone?

CONCLUSION: LEAVING A LASTING LEGACY

Daniel's success as Vice President came from his ability to balance vision with execution, lead through uncertainty, and drive results that supported the company's long-term objectives. By fostering innovation, developing his senior leaders, and ensuring alignment across functions, he built a legacy of operational excellence that positioned the company for sustained success. His leadership exemplifies what it means to operate at the highest levels—guiding not just teams or departments, but the future of the entire organization.

As a Vice President or beyond, your success comes from your ability to lead with vision, manage complexity, and drive long-term success for the company. At this level, leadership is about leaving a lasting legacy—shaping the future of the business, developing the next generation of leaders, and ensuring that the company is positioned for continued growth and innovation.

Part 4:

Timeless Leadership Principles

FROM FOUNDATION TO MASTERY:
THE SKILLS THAT ELEVATE LEADERS AT EVERY STAGE

As you progress through your leadership journey, the foundation built in Parts 1, 2, and 3—excelling as an individual contributor, mastering people management, and learning to run a business—prepares you for the final phase of leadership mastery. Part 4, *Timeless Leadership Principles*, shifts the focus to essential, enduring skills that differentiate good leaders from great ones. These principles not only elevate your performance but also ensure that you sustain success across every stage of your career.

Each chapter in this section highlights a critical leadership trait, skill, or practice that leaders must continually refine. These are the timeless qualities that make the difference between merely advancing through the ranks and becoming an exceptional leader who leaves a lasting legacy.

In previous sections, we examined how success at the individual and managerial levels (Parts 1 and 2) depends on building a strong foundation of reliability, communication, and strategic influence. As we moved into running a business in Part 3, we explored how vision, strategy, and operational excellence become critical in shaping an organization's success. Now, in Part 4, we turn our attention to the timeless principles that sustain leadership excellence through the complexities of growth, change, and long-term impact.

These are the key skills that every leader, regardless of role, needs to cultivate and apply consistently:

1. **Vision, Strategy, and Goals** (Chapter 11) explores the importance of leading with purpose, focusing on setting a clear direction and aligning strategy with action.

2. **Networking** (Chapter 12) emphasizes the power of building relationships at every stage of your career, showcasing how influence is as much about who you know as what you know.

3. **Disagree and Commit** (Chapter 13) delves into conflict management, teaching leaders how to navigate disagreements constructively and foster team commitment once decisions are made.

4. **Extroversion, Assertiveness, and Confidence** (Chapter 14) highlights the importance of leading with presence, regardless of personality type, and mastering assertiveness to inspire trust and decisiveness.

5. **Office Politics** (Chapter 15) acknowledges the reality of power dynamics in organizations, guiding leaders on how to navigate influence ethically and build alliances without compromising values.

6. **Humility** (Chapter 16) focuses on leading with empathy and recognizing the equal value of every individual in the organization, ensuring that leadership is grounded in respect, self-awareness, and the success of others.

REINFORCING LESSONS FROM EARLIER PARTS

The timeless leadership principles in this final section tie directly back to the lessons you've learned so far. At the entry-level and mid-level stages (Part 1), success came from executing your tasks well and building your sphere of influence through relationships and trust. As you moved into managing people (Part 2), it became clear that leadership wasn't just about your personal performance—it was about how well you could inspire and guide others to meet collective goals.

Running a business (Part 3) required you to develop a strategic vision, manage complexity, and drive long-term results.

Now, in Part 4, these principles become critical as you learn how to consistently apply vision, communication, conflict resolution, and humility to excel as a leader. Let's break this down further:

- **Vision, Strategy, and Goals**: In Part 3, we explored how vision and strategy are the foundation of running a successful business. Now, you'll deepen your understanding by learning how to articulate these concepts clearly, inspire your team, and align every action to long-term goals. Whether you're leading a small project or an entire department, having a clear direction and the ability to rally others behind it is essential.

- **Networking**: Building relationships is a skill you've practiced throughout your career, as discussed in Part 1 when forming a foundation and in Part 2 while managing teams. Networking is not only about expanding your influence within your company but also about leveraging your connections to support your personal and professional growth.

- **Disagree and Commit**: As we explored in Part 2, managing people means balancing competing priorities and navigating conflict. In Part 3, you saw how leading complex business functions requires collaboration and managing disagreements. This chapter will show you how to use conflict as a tool for stronger decisions and deeper commitment to shared goals.

- **Extroversion, Assertiveness, and Confidence**: Whether you're an introvert or extrovert, leading with confidence and decisiveness is critical at every stage. In Part 3, you learned how senior leaders like Emily, Amanda, and Daniel used their presence to command respect and drive results. Now, we'll explore how to cultivate that presence and develop the assertiveness needed to influence others effectively.

- **Office Politics**: Throughout your career, from entry-level to senior leadership, navigating organizational dynamics has been a part of your success. Part 4 teaches you how to engage with office politics ethically—building alliances and managing power dynamics without compromising your values, ensuring that your contributions are recognized while maintaining integrity.

- **Humility**: Leadership, as we've seen throughout this book, is ultimately about people. From mentoring junior employees to managing teams or leading a business, the most successful leaders stay grounded in humility. In this chapter, you'll learn how to balance confidence with empathy, recognizing that true leadership is about empowering others and fostering a culture of respect.

ELEVATING LEADERSHIP ACROSS EVERY MILESTONE

The principles in this final section are not just concepts to be learned—they are habits to be practiced at every stage of your career. Whether you're at the start of your leadership journey or navigating the complexities of executive roles, these principles will ensure that you remain effective, adaptable, and impactful.

By the time you finish Part 4, you'll have a comprehensive toolkit for leading with integrity, confidence, and purpose. You'll understand how to align vision with strategy, build influential networks, manage conflict, assert your leadership presence, and navigate office dynamics—all while leading with humility and respect for those around you.

These timeless principles are what separate good leaders from great ones. Mastering them will ensure that you continue to break boundaries, not just in your career but in the lives of the people you lead.

Now, let's dive into the first principle: leading with vision, strategy, and clear goals to ensure that every step you take aligns with your greater purpose.

Chapter 11:

Vision, Strategy, and Goals – Leading with Purpose

On stage before a large audience, Robert inspires employees by connecting the company's vision to strategic goals. His powerful presentation reflects the unity of purpose and leadership.

INTRODUCTION: SETTING THE FOUNDATION OF LEADERSHIP

At the core of great leadership lies one fundamental truth: without a clear vision, strategy, and set of goals, you and your team are simply wandering. Vision is the compass that sets the direction, strategy is the map that details the journey, and goals are the milestones that measure progress along the way. Whether you are managing a small team or leading an entire company, understanding how to define and execute these key elements is essential to long-term success.

In previous chapters, we explored how a leader's role evolves as you rise through the ranks. From an entry-level individual contributor (Chapter 1) to senior management (Chapter 6), your ability to articulate a clear vision, develop a thoughtful strategy, and set achievable goals becomes increasingly critical. Without these foundational elements, even the most well-intentioned teams can find themselves off-course, struggling to deliver results or move forward with purpose.

But what exactly are vision, strategy, and goals—and just as important—what are they not? In this chapter, we'll define each concept, explore their characteristics, and provide examples of how they can either drive success or lead to missed opportunities.

VISION: DEFINING THE DESTINATION

A clear vision is the cornerstone of effective leadership. It's the big picture that inspires action, aligns teams, and gives meaning to the work being done. Vision answers the fundamental question: *Where are we going?* It paints a picture of the future that the team or organization aspires to achieve, giving purpose to daily tasks and long-term projects alike.

What Vision Is:

- **Inspiration and Direction:** A well-crafted vision is both inspirational and directional. It isn't just about stating a goal; it's about setting an aspirational target that motivates everyone involved. Think of it as a guiding star—while the specifics of the journey may shift, the overall direction remains the same.

- **Long-Term Focus:** Vision is inherently long-term. It reflects what you want the team or organization to become, not just what it needs to do in the short term. For example, Steve Jobs famously envisioned Apple not just as a computer company but as an innovative force in technology and design.

- **Motivating and Energizing:** Vision provides the "why" behind the work. It's what gets people excited to come to work each day and drives them to overcome challenges.

What Vision Is Not:

- **A Checklist of Tasks:** Vision is not a to-do list or a series of operational tasks. While execution is important, vision is about the overarching direction, not the day-to-day details.

- **Vague or Generic Statements:** A strong vision is specific and compelling. It's not enough to say, "We want to be the best in the industry." What does that look like? How will you get there? A generic statement lacks the depth and inspiration needed to rally a team.

Example of Vision Done Right: When Elon Musk founded SpaceX, his vision wasn't just to build rockets—it was to enable humans to live on other planets. This bold, audacious vision energized his team, attracted top talent, and provided clear long-term direction for the company. Every project at SpaceX ties back to that core vision, ensuring that even the most technical details serve a higher purpose.

Example of Vision Gone Wrong: Contrast this with a mid-sized tech company that set a vision to "grow revenues by 20%." While that's an admirable goal, it lacks the inspirational quality of a true vision. It's a financial target, not a direction. Without a larger, purpose-driven vision, the company's efforts became fragmented, and the team struggled to stay motivated. Growth stalled, and the company eventually had to rethink its entire strategy.

STRATEGY: THE ROADMAP TO SUCCESS

If vision is the destination, strategy is the roadmap. A strategy is how you plan to get from where you are today to where your vision tells you to go. It's the bridge between the aspirational future you've defined and the current reality your team operates in. While a vision might be broad, a strategy needs to be concrete, practical, and actionable.

What Strategy Is:

- **A Plan for Achieving the Vision:** Strategy provides a framework for making decisions. It lays out the key initiatives, resources, and actions necessary to move toward the vision. Without strategy, teams are left guessing how to prioritize their efforts.

- **Focused and Cohesive:** Strategy isn't about doing everything. It's about making choices. A good strategy focuses on the most impactful actions that will drive progress toward the vision. As we discussed in Chapter 4.5, when stepping into management, learning to prioritize is key to your success as a leader.

- **Adaptive to Change:** While the vision remains relatively constant, strategy must be flexible. The best strategies allow for course corrections when new information or challenges arise.

What Strategy Is Not:

- **A Static Document:** Strategy is not something you create once and never revisit. Market conditions change, new opportunities emerge, and unforeseen challenges arise. A successful strategy evolves over time.

- **Overly Detailed or Micromanaged Plans:** While it's important to have a clear roadmap, a strategy that tries to account for every minor detail can become restrictive. Instead of micromanaging every step, the strategy should provide high-level direction and allow for flexibility in execution.

Example of Strategy Done Right: A retail company might have a vision to be "the most customer-centric brand in the market." To achieve this, the strategy could focus on three pillars: exceptional customer service, innovative product offerings, and a seamless omnichannel shopping experience. The strategy details the key initiatives under each pillar—such as investing in customer service training, launching new digital platforms, and expanding the product line. This gives the company a clear, focused plan while allowing flexibility in execution as customer needs evolve.

Example of Strategy Gone Wrong: On the other hand, a strategy that tries to tackle too many things at once is doomed to fail. A company with a vision to "lead the market in innovation" but a strategy that includes too many conflicting initiatives—expansion, cost-cutting, product diversification, entering new markets—can easily lose focus.

By spreading resources too thin and pulling the team in multiple directions, the company risks making little progress on any front. This is a classic case of strategy lacking focus.

GOALS: THE MILESTONES ALONG THE WAY

Goals are the specific, measurable milestones that help you track progress toward your vision and execute your strategy. They provide clarity, keep the team focused, and create a sense of accountability. While the vision is long-term and the strategy is high-level, goals break everything down into actionable, short- and medium-term targets.

What Goals Are:

- **Specific, Measurable Targets:** Goals are concrete and measurable. They provide clarity on what success looks like at each stage of the journey. A well-defined goal is specific— "increase customer satisfaction by 10% within the next 6 months"—and easy to track.

- **Short- to Medium-Term Focus:** While the vision is long-term, goals should be short- to medium-term, guiding day-to-day efforts. These might be quarterly sales targets, product launch timelines, or operational efficiency improvements.

- **Aligned with Vision and Strategy:** Every goal should directly contribute to achieving the broader vision and fit within the overall strategy. Goals that don't align will lead to confusion and fragmented efforts.

What Goals Are Not:

- **Ambiguous or Vague Aspirations:** Goals that are not measurable are ineffective. Statements like "improve teamwork" or "be more innovative" are well-meaning, but without clear, measurable targets, they lack the specificity needed to drive action.

- **A To-Do List:** Goals should not be confused with task lists. While tasks are important for execution, goals focus on outcomes and results, not just activities.

Example of Goals Done Right: Consider an HR department tasked with improving employee engagement. Instead of saying, "Make employees happier," they set a specific goal: "Increase employee engagement scores by 15% over the next 12 months by improving communication, recognition programs, and career development opportunities." This goal is measurable, aligned with the company's vision for a positive workplace culture, and ties directly to strategic initiatives like improving internal communication and retention.

Example of Goals Gone Wrong: A bad example of goal setting might be a company with a vision to "become the leader in sustainability" but sets vague or conflicting goals like "reduce costs" without specifying how it relates to their sustainability efforts. Without clarity or alignment between goals and vision, the company risks undermining its core values.

TYING IT ALL TOGETHER:
THE VISION-STRATEGY-GOAL CONTINUUM

Effective leadership means understanding how vision, strategy, and goals work together. Vision defines where you're headed, strategy outlines how you'll get there, and goals provide the roadmap for progress along the way. These three elements must be aligned for your team to stay focused and motivated, avoiding the pitfalls of fragmented efforts and unclear direction.

In earlier chapters, especially Chapter 4 on team leadership and Chapter 6 on senior management, we discussed how managing both the details and the big picture is crucial as you move through leadership roles. By now, you should have a solid understanding of how to craft these key elements, ensuring that your team or organization stays on course toward long-term success.

CONCLUSION: LEADING WITH PURPOSE

Vision, strategy, and goals are not just abstract concepts—they are the foundation of leadership at every level. Whether you're leading a small team or steering an entire organization, your ability to define a compelling vision, craft a thoughtful strategy, and set actionable goals will determine your success. Great leaders don't just manage tasks; they inspire, strategize, and guide their teams toward a meaningful, impactful future.

In the next chapter, we'll explore another key leadership principle: building and leveraging networks. The relationships you build within and outside of your organization are essential to achieving your vision, executing your strategy, and realizing your goals.

Chapter 12:

Networking – Building Relationships for Success

At a professional mixer, Robert exchanges ideas and handshakes with other leaders. His ease in fostering connections highlights the critical role of relationships in his success.

INTRODUCTION: THE POWER OF NETWORKING AT EVERY LEVEL

Success in leadership doesn't happen in isolation. No matter how skilled or dedicated you are, your ability to build and nurture meaningful relationships will ultimately determine how far you can go in your career. Networking is not just about meeting influential people or shaking hands at events; it's about building a community of trusted individuals who can support, guide, and open doors for you throughout your professional journey.

Whether you're an entry-level employee just starting out or a senior director shaping the future of a department, your network is your greatest asset. In Chapter 4, we discussed how leaders begin to expand their sphere of influence as they move into managerial roles. Here, we'll explore how that influence is built and sustained through strategic networking at every level of your career.

Building a network is something you should start right away. If you're early in your career, begin forming relationships immediately with peers, managers, and colleagues across departments. As you grow, that network will serve as a source of mentorship, collaboration, and opportunity.

THE THREE TYPES OF CONNECTIONS IN YOUR NETWORK

Before diving into networking strategies, it's essential to recognize that not all connections are created equal. Your professional network is made up of different types of relationships, and understanding how to build, cultivate, and leverage them effectively will allow you to make the most of your interactions.

1. Strong Connections – People You've Worked With or For:

These are the people who know your work firsthand. They've seen you in action, either as a peer, direct report, or supervisor. These relationships are the most valuable because they are built on trust and experience. Strong connections know your capabilities, strengths, and how you handle challenges. These individuals are more likely to advocate for you when opportunities arise because they've seen your work ethic and character up close.

For example, in Chapter 5, we saw how Maria expanded her influence as she transitioned into management by strengthening relationships with other managers and department heads. Those connections were built on her reputation for delivering results and supporting her team, which positioned her as a trusted leader within the organization.

2. Weak Connections – Acquaintances and Distant Colleagues:
These are people you've met briefly at events or interacted with online but haven't worked with directly. While they may be useful for expanding your network and gaining insights into different industries or companies, these connections are more transactional in nature. They might not know your work well enough to vouch for you, but they can still provide useful information, recommendations, or introductions.

3. Online Connections – People You Connect with on Platforms Like LinkedIn:
With tools like LinkedIn, X/Twitter, and other professional social platforms, it's easier than ever to connect with people in your industry, from thought leaders to potential clients. However, online connections are only as valuable as the relationships you build after the initial "connect." Simply adding someone to your LinkedIn network doesn't mean you've established a meaningful connection. You need to engage with them, follow up with insights, and turn a digital relationship into a professional one.

Treating Different Connections Differently:
Understanding these differences helps you approach each group in a way that nurtures relationships. Strong connections require ongoing

engagement and mutual support, while weak or online connections may need more effort to develop into something meaningful. The key is to be intentional—don't treat your network as a collection of names, but as a community of people with whom you share genuine professional relationships.

HOW TO BUILD STRATEGIC RELATIONSHIPS FROM DAY ONE

It's never too early—or too late—to start building your network. Whether you're in your first job or decades into your career, developing relationships with colleagues, peers, mentors, and industry professionals should be a continuous process. Here are some techniques for building a professional network at different stages of your career:

1. Build Relationships Across All Levels

Networking isn't just about connecting with senior leaders. In fact, many of the most valuable connections you'll make are with peers or colleagues at your level. As we discussed in Chapter 1, even entry-level professionals can begin forming relationships that will serve them later in their career. Some of your peers will rise alongside you, becoming managers, directors, and executives themselves. Nurturing those early connections can lead to long-lasting alliances.

It's also important to build connections with those in junior roles. Leaders who help develop talent are often remembered fondly and may find future opportunities from those they once mentored.

2. Be Curious and Show Interest in Others

One of the best ways to start building a relationship is by showing genuine curiosity in someone's work, career path, or industry. Ask questions about what they do, what they're passionate about, and the challenges they face. This demonstrates that you value their insights and aren't just looking to advance your own career.

For instance, if you're a new manager, you can start by engaging other managers or directors across different departments, learning about their goals and challenges, and finding common ground. These conversations can lead to collaborations, mentorship opportunities, or support when you need it.

3. Network Outside Your Department

It's easy to stay within the confines of your department or team, but real networking happens when you step outside your immediate circle. Attend cross-functional meetings, participate in company events, and engage with colleagues from other areas of the organization. The more diverse your network, the more perspectives and opportunities you'll gain.

Maria, for instance, built a strong cross-departmental network by attending meetings in marketing, product development, and customer success. This broadened her understanding of the business and helped her develop relationships that would be crucial as she advanced in her career.

4. Leverage Tools Like LinkedIn and X/Twitter

While online platforms shouldn't replace face-to-face networking, they can be powerful tools for connecting with professionals you might not otherwise meet. LinkedIn, for example, allows you to not only connect with colleagues but also join professional groups, participate in discussions, and engage with content shared by leaders in your field.

However, don't stop at connecting. After meeting someone online, follow up with a message that demonstrates you're interested in building a meaningful relationship. Share an article they might find useful, comment on their work, or suggest a virtual coffee meeting to exchange ideas.

On platforms like X/Twitter, engage with industry conversations, share your own insights, and connect with thought leaders by responding to their tweets or starting a dialogue. This positions you as someone who is active and engaged in the industry, not just a passive observer.

5. Broaching Networking in Conversation

Networking doesn't have to feel transactional or forced. Often, the best connections are made organically through genuine interactions. Here's how you can broach networking in conversation:

- **Compliment their work:** If you've read a report, article, or seen a presentation from someone you admire, reach out and mention how it impacted your thinking or work.

- **Ask for advice:** People love sharing their expertise. Asking for advice on a career move, project, or challenge is a great way to start a conversation. Make it clear that you respect their opinion.

- **Follow up after events or meetings:** If you meet someone at an event or in a cross-departmental meeting, send a quick follow-up message thanking them for the interaction and suggesting future collaboration.

BUILDING STRATEGIC ALLIANCES: LEVERAGING YOUR NETWORK FOR SUCCESS

As you progress in your career, it's essential to not just grow your network, but to strategically leverage it. This means forming alliances with key stakeholders who can help you drive projects forward, open new opportunities, or provide support when needed. Strategic alliances are built on trust, collaboration, and shared goals.

1. Identify Key Stakeholders

The first step in building strategic alliances is identifying the individuals who have influence over the areas you're trying to impact. These might be senior leaders, cross-functional colleagues, or even external partners. It's not just about "networking up"—often, peers or team members from other departments are equally valuable.

2. Collaborate on Projects

One of the best ways to solidify a relationship is by working together on a project or initiative. Collaboration builds trust, highlights your strengths, and opens the door for future opportunities. By working with others to achieve shared objectives, you position yourself as a team player and a leader who knows how to build alliances for success.

3. Be a Connector

Leaders who make a habit of connecting others are often seen as valuable networkers. If you know two people who could benefit from working together, make an introduction. By facilitating valuable connections within your network, you not only help others succeed but also position yourself as someone with a strong, interconnected network.

BUILDING YOUR PERSONAL BRAND: STANDING OUT IN YOUR NETWORK

A strong personal brand is what sets you apart in the minds of others. It's how people remember you, what they associate you with, and what they value about your contributions. In Chapter 7, we talked about the importance of being a visionary leader. Building a personal brand is one way to ensure that people recognize you as a leader in your field.

1. Define Your Core Values

Start by identifying the core values that drive your leadership and professional behavior. Are you known for your integrity, innovation, problem-solving skills, or ability to develop others? Your personal brand should reflect the values you want others to associate with you.

2. Be Consistent in Your Actions and Communication

Consistency is key to building a strong personal brand. If you want to be known for innovation, continuously seek out new ways to solve problems and share those ideas with your network. If you want to be known for supporting others, be generous with your time and insights, mentoring others and contributing to their success.

3. Share Your Expertise

One way to build a strong personal brand is by sharing your expertise through articles, presentations, or social media content. This positions you as a thought leader in your field and helps people associate your name with valuable insights. Whether it's through LinkedIn posts, speaking at conferences, or publishing industry articles, sharing your knowledge can significantly strengthen your personal brand.

4. Align Your Brand with Your Network's Needs

As you build your personal brand, think about how it aligns with the needs and interests of your network. If you work in a fast-evolving field like technology, focus on being seen as someone who's always ahead of industry trends. If your field values collaboration, highlight your ability to build strong teams and relationships.

CONCLUSION: YOUR NETWORK IS YOUR GREATEST ASSET

The relationships you build, nurture, and leverage will define your leadership journey as much as your own skills and abilities. Whether you're just starting out or sitting in a senior leadership role, the power of your network cannot be overstated. Building strong, genuine connections, forming strategic alliances, and shaping your personal brand will provide you with the tools to navigate challenges, seize opportunities, and ultimately, achieve success.

In the next chapter, we'll explore the importance of navigating disagreement and commitment, and how mastering conflict resolution can elevate your leadership.

Chapter 13:

Disagree and Commit – Leading Through Conflict

Faced with a disagreement between two executives, Robert mediates calmly and decisively. His leadership ensures conflicts resolve into actionable commitments.

INTRODUCTION: THE ART OF HEALTHY DISAGREEMENT

Leadership is not about avoiding conflict or blindly following the decisions of others—it's about navigating disagreement with grace, wisdom, and purpose. At every level of leadership, conflict will arise. Whether it's a difference of opinion on strategy, competing priorities, or varied perspectives on how to achieve a common goal, healthy conflict is essential to progress. How you handle disagreement will define not only your leadership style but also the culture of the team or organization you lead.

In this chapter, we'll explore the principle of "disagree and commit," a leadership technique that encourages open debate but ultimately fosters unity once a decision is made. It's a practice that allows leaders to voice their concerns, advocate for their ideas, and fully commit to decisions—even when they don't agree with them. Beyond this, we'll examine the psychology of decision-making in leadership and how different factors, from experience to instinct, shape the choices leaders make. Ultimately, effective leadership requires knowing when to push back, when to stand your ground, and how to commit fully to the team's direction once a decision is made.

THE PSYCHOLOGY OF DECISION-MAKING IN LEADERSHIP

At the heart of every disagreement is the process of decision-making. Understanding how leaders come to decisions—and how these decisions are influenced by factors like experience, emotions, and instinct—can help you better navigate conflict and disagreement.

According to research on leadership psychology, decision-making is rarely based solely on objective facts. Leaders draw from a variety of influences:

- **Experience:** Seasoned leaders often make decisions based on patterns they've seen before. They rely on past successes and failures to guide their current choices. For example, a CEO who has successfully navigated through an economic downturn may feel confident in taking decisive action during a future recession, based on prior experience.

- **Emotions:** Leaders are human, and emotions inevitably play a role in decision-making. Whether it's passion for a particular project, frustration with roadblocks, or fear of failure, emotions can sway how leaders evaluate options and choose a path forward. Emotional intelligence is key here—great leaders recognize their emotions and understand how to manage them when making decisions.

- **Instinct or Gut Feeling:** Particularly in fast-moving environments or situations with incomplete data, leaders often rely on intuition to make decisions. This "gut feeling" is often rooted in a combination of experience and subconscious processing. A marketing director, for instance, may choose a new campaign strategy based on instinct, even if the data isn't fully clear.

Understanding these influences can help you navigate disagreements with leaders more effectively. If a decision is based on experience, it may be worth questioning whether past conditions still apply to the current situation. If emotions are driving a decision, acknowledging those emotions can lead to a more balanced discussion. If it's instinct, you may need to rely on data or evidence to offer an alternative perspective.

Example of the Psychology at Play: Imagine you're part of a leadership team considering whether to pursue a risky but innovative product launch. The CEO, relying on her instinct and past success with similar risks, pushes hard for the launch. However, the CFO, driven by his experience during the last economic downturn, expresses concern over financial exposure. The CMO, meanwhile, is emotionally invested in the project and argues passionately for it. This mix of experience, emotion, and instinct creates tension, but understanding these influences helps you navigate the conversation and ultimately reach a well-rounded decision.

DISAGREE AND COMMIT:
THE FRAMEWORK FOR PRODUCTIVE CONFLICT

The principle of "disagree and commit" originated in corporate cultures like Amazon, where leaders are encouraged to engage in open debate and express their honest opinions. However, once a decision is made—even if you don't fully agree with it—you commit wholeheartedly to its success. This allows for healthy conflict and debate without creating division or ongoing friction within the team.

Here's how "disagree and commit" works in practice:

1. **Voice Your Perspective Clearly:** When you disagree with a proposed decision, it's important to express your concerns respectfully and constructively. Present your reasoning with supporting evidence, drawing on data, insights, or experiences that back up your point of view. This ensures that your disagreement isn't personal or emotional but grounded in facts and logic.
   For example, if you disagree with a strategic direction because you believe the market conditions are unfavorable, present relevant data and insights to support your position. It's not enough to say "I don't like this idea"—you need to explain *why*.

2. **Engage in Constructive Debate:** Healthy disagreement fosters better decisions. Engaging in open, respectful

debate allows the team to explore different perspectives and potentially arrive at a more nuanced solution. However, it's essential to remain professional and focused on the issue, not the individuals involved. Personal attacks or dismissive attitudes undermine productive conflict.

3. **Know When to Pick Your Battles:** Not every disagreement needs to turn into a prolonged debate. Part of being a good leader is knowing when to stand your ground and when to yield. Consider the stakes—how important is the issue in the grand scheme of things? Will this decision significantly impact the team's success, or is it a minor point of contention?

   Your ability to push back, and how hard you push, will depend on your history, performance, and the trust you've built with leadership. If you've consistently delivered results and proven your value, your concerns will carry more weight. On the other hand, pushing too hard on every issue can make you appear combative or resistant to collaboration.

4. **Once a Decision is Made, Commit Fully:** This is the critical part of the "disagree and commit" framework. Once a decision is made—whether or not you agree with it—you need to let go of the disagreement and fully commit to the team's direction. Continuing to argue your point after the decision is finalized only creates division. The goal is to align the entire team toward executing the decision as effectively as possible.

   Example of Disagree and Commit: Sarah, a project manager, disagrees with her leadership's decision to allocate resources to a lower-priority project. She believes the focus should be on another initiative that will have a higher return. During the leadership meeting, she presents her case, citing data and metrics that support her recommendation. After some debate, the decision is made to go forward with the original plan. Although Sarah disagrees, she commits fully to making the chosen project successful, ensuring that her team delivers on time and to the best of their ability. Her willingness to commit despite her disagreement builds trust and shows her alignment with the team.

FOSTERING A CULTURE OF CONSTRUCTIVE CONFLICT

Leaders who are able to foster an environment where conflict is viewed as a healthy part of decision-making will ultimately lead more successful teams. Conflict, when handled properly, leads to better decisions, stronger outcomes, and a culture where diverse perspectives are valued.

In earlier chapters, particularly Chapter 7 on senior management, we discussed how leaders must manage complexity and navigate through competing priorities. Encouraging constructive conflict is one way to ensure that diverse perspectives are heard and that leaders don't operate in an echo chamber.

Here are some strategies to build a culture where constructive conflict thrives:

1. Create Psychological Safety:

Psychological safety refers to creating an environment where team members feel comfortable expressing their opinions, ideas, and disagreements without fear of retribution or embarrassment. Leaders can foster this by encouraging open dialogue, showing respect for differing viewpoints, and being transparent in their decision-making processes. If team members feel safe to voice their concerns, disagreements are more likely to be productive.

2. Normalize Disagreement:

Leaders must demonstrate that disagreement is not only accepted but valued. Openly challenge ideas (in a respectful manner) and invite others to do the same. This can be achieved through regular brainstorming sessions where differing opinions are encouraged, or by playing "devil's advocate" to ensure all sides of an argument are explored.

3. Establish Ground Rules for Conflict:

Not all conflict is constructive. Setting clear expectations for how disagreements should be handled can prevent conversations from devolving into personal attacks or counterproductive arguments. Leaders should encourage their teams to focus on the issue, not the person, and to back up their positions with evidence rather than emotion.

4. Reward Healthy Conflict:

A great way to reinforce the value of constructive conflict is to recognize and reward it. Celebrate when a team member offers a dissenting opinion that leads to a better outcome. This reinforces the idea that disagreement is not a problem—it's a solution in progress.

Example of Fostering Constructive Conflict: At an advertising agency, the creative team and the accounts team often clashed over project timelines. Rather than allowing these disagreements to create division, the agency's leadership decided to host monthly "collision meetings" where each department aired their concerns and worked through disagreements in a structured environment. These meetings gave both sides a platform to voice their perspectives, and over time, the teams developed a deeper respect for each other's needs. As a result, the agency produced more creative, innovative campaigns that balanced the needs of both departments.

KNOWING WHEN TO PUSH BACK AND WHEN TO PIVOT

One of the most important skills in leadership is knowing when to push back and how hard to stand your ground. It's critical to pick your battles wisely and understand when it's time to yield. As we've discussed throughout this book, your history, performance, and relationship with leadership will influence how far you can push in a disagreement.

Trust and Credibility: Your ability to disagree effectively—and be heard—often depends on the trust and credibility you've built over time. If you've consistently delivered results, shown good judgment, and earned the respect of your peers and leadership, your opinion will carry more weight. This doesn't mean you should only speak up when you're certain you'll get your way, but it does mean that if you've established yourself as a trusted leader, people will listen when you disagree.

Pivoting When You're Wrong: Equally important is the ability to pivot when you realize you were wrong. Strong leaders are not stubborn; they're adaptable. If the decision you initially disagreed with starts to show results, acknowledge it. Admitting you were wrong shows maturity, self-awareness, and a commitment to the team's success over your personal ego.

CONCLUSION: LEADERSHIP IS BUILT THROUGH CONSTRUCTIVE CONFLICT

Disagreement is not something to fear—it's something to embrace as part of a healthy leadership dynamic. By mastering the art of "disagree and commit," you can navigate conflict effectively, advocate for your ideas, and help your team or organization make better decisions. More importantly, fostering a culture where constructive conflict is encouraged will lead to stronger performance, mutual respect, and better outcomes across the board.

In the next chapter, we'll explore how to build and maintain the confidence, assertiveness, and extroversion needed to lead effectively, even in the face of opposition or conflict.

Chapter 14:

Extroversion, Assertiveness, and Confidence – Leading with Presence

Robert delivers a commanding speech at a podium, capturing the audience's attention. His confident presence demonstrates how assertiveness enhances leadership impact.

INTRODUCTION: FINDING YOUR LEADERSHIP VOICE

Leadership is not about who talks the most, who commands the loudest room, or who seems to have the most charisma. True leadership presence is about being heard when it matters most. Whether you're naturally introverted or extroverted, confident or cautious, you can learn to project the kind of assertiveness and presence that inspires trust and drives action. Leadership is about making an impact without losing authenticity, and the key to developing this lies in finding your unique leadership voice.

In this chapter, we will explore how introversion and extroversion work, and how both personality types can lead effectively. We'll also focus on the critical role of assertiveness and confidence in leadership, and how developing an executive presence will enable you to influence others, make strong decisions, and deliver results. Building on earlier discussions around decision-making and conflict resolution (see Chapter 12), we'll emphasize how confidence and decisiveness are key to earning trust and pushing initiatives forward—especially when the path is unclear.

INTROVERSION VS. EXTROVERSION:
THE PSYCHOLOGY BEHIND YOUR LEADERSHIP STYLE

A common misconception about leadership is that extroversion equates to better leadership, while introversion is a barrier to success. In reality, both introverts and extroverts can thrive as leaders—what matters is how you leverage your natural tendencies to influence others and project confidence.

Understanding the Difference:

- **Extroversion** is often characterized by energy gained from social interaction, outward enthusiasm, and a preference for collaboration. Extroverts tend to thrive in group settings and may speak or act spontaneously. They draw energy from external stimuli and are often seen as assertive and outgoing.

- **Introversion**, on the other hand, is characterized by a preference for quieter, more controlled environments and introspection. Introverts tend to feel drained by prolonged social interaction and often need time alone to recharge. This doesn't mean they dislike people or aren't social, but rather, they find their energy in reflection and focused, deliberate interaction.

Importantly, introversion and extroversion exist on a spectrum. Most people fall somewhere in between, exhibiting traits of both. Leadership doesn't belong to one group over the other—rather, it's about understanding your tendencies and knowing when and how to apply them.

Introverts as Leaders: Introverts often excel in roles that require deep thinking, careful listening, and thoughtful decision-making. Many introverted leaders have an innate ability to observe, listen, and absorb different viewpoints before arriving at a decision. They are also known for their ability to build deep, meaningful relationships, which can foster trust and loyalty among team members.

Extroverts as Leaders: Extroverted leaders bring energy, enthusiasm, and a natural ability to connect with large groups of people. They are often comfortable taking the lead in high-energy environments, motivating their teams with verbal encouragement and charisma. Their challenge lies in balancing outward energy with the need for reflection and measured decision-making.

PROJECTING CONFIDENCE:
ASSERTIVENESS WITHOUT LOSING AUTHENTICITY

Leadership presence comes down to one key trait: confidence. Whether you're naturally extroverted or introverted, you can develop the ability to project confidence and assertiveness. Confidence doesn't mean pretending to have all the answers, but rather, trusting yourself to navigate uncertainty and take calculated risks.

In previous chapters, especially when we discussed conflict resolution (Chapter 12) and decision-making (Chapter 10), we explored how decisiveness and the ability to commit to a course of action are central to building trust as a leader. Confidence is the foundation of that decisiveness.

What Confidence Is:

- **Belief in Your Own Judgment:** Confidence comes from knowing you are capable of making informed decisions, even in uncertain situations. It's not about having all the answers upfront but trusting that you can navigate challenges as they arise.

- **Projecting Assurance:** Whether you're presenting an idea in a meeting or negotiating a major deal, projecting confidence—both verbally and through body language—helps others believe in your ability to lead. It's important to note that confidence can be quietly strong. A calm, assured demeanor can be just as effective as outward enthusiasm.

What Confidence Is Not:

- **Overconfidence or Arrogance:** Confidence does not mean you dismiss other perspectives or act without considering the consequences. Leaders who project overconfidence often ignore important feedback, which can lead to poor decisions and loss of trust.

- **Faking It:** Some mistakenly believe that confidence means "faking it until you make it." While a positive mindset is important, authenticity is crucial. Confidence should come from a place of genuine competence and understanding, not from a manufactured persona.

Assertiveness: The Balance Between Respect and Authority

Assertiveness is the ability to express your ideas, needs, or boundaries clearly while respecting others. It's about speaking up for yourself and your team in a way that commands attention but doesn't dominate the conversation. This is especially important for introverted leaders, who may feel hesitant to assert themselves in louder environments.

Techniques for Building Assertiveness:

1. **Know Your Value:** Understand what you bring to the table, whether it's technical expertise, strategic thinking, or strong team-building skills. When you know your value, it becomes easier to assert yourself when necessary.

2. **Frame Your Ideas Positively:** Assertiveness is not about being confrontational. It's about framing your ideas in a way that aligns with the group's goals. Use language like, "I believe this will help us achieve X," or "Here's how we can address this challenge together."

3. **Practice Saying No:** Leaders often struggle with setting boundaries, especially in high-pressure environments. Being

assertive includes saying no when necessary—whether it's to an unreasonable deadline, an off-target project, or even a higher-up's suggestion that doesn't align with your team's goals.

DECISIVENESS: THE KEY TO BUILDING TRUST AND DELIVERING RESULTS

Confidence in leadership is closely tied to decisiveness. The ability to make decisions, especially when the path is not entirely clear, is what earns trust from both your team and senior leaders. Indecisiveness creates uncertainty, erodes confidence, and can stall progress. On the other hand, decisive leaders are able to weigh options, consider risks, and make informed decisions—even under pressure.

Why Decisiveness Matters:

1. **It Builds Trust:** When you consistently make decisions—whether they turn out to be right or wrong—you build trust with your team and superiors. People know they can count on you to take action and lead the way forward. As discussed in Chapter 6, senior managers must often make decisions in the face of ambiguity, and those decisions can make or break the trust of their teams.

2. **It Moves Teams Forward:** In business, inaction is often worse than making a wrong decision. Decisiveness keeps projects moving, prevents paralysis by analysis, and ensures that momentum isn't lost. As discussed in Chapter 10 on vision and strategy, the ability to move from strategy to execution often depends on clear decision-making.

3. **It Demonstrates Leadership Under Pressure:** Great leaders aren't those who make perfect decisions every time—they

are those who make decisions with confidence and adapt when things don't go as planned. In fast-moving business environments, leaders who wait too long for the "right" information can miss opportunities. As we've discussed throughout the book, taking calculated risks is a hallmark of leadership growth.

Example of Decisiveness in Action: Daniel, a mid-level manager at a growing tech firm, was tasked with deciding between two software vendors for a major project. Both options had pros and cons, and the data wasn't conclusive. Instead of delaying the project by waiting for more information, Daniel made the decision to move forward with one vendor, based on the team's feedback and his own analysis. The project launched successfully, and even though there were challenges, his decisiveness kept the team moving forward, which earned him praise from senior leadership.

DEVELOPING EXECUTIVE PRESENCE: COMMANDING RESPECT AND ATTENTION

Executive presence is about more than just looking the part. It's about how you carry yourself, how you communicate, and how you engage with others in high-stakes situations. People with executive presence don't need to be the most vocal, but they are the ones who command attention when they speak.

As you grow into leadership roles—whether as a manager, director, or beyond—developing executive presence becomes essential. It's not just about making decisions; it's about influencing others, rallying teams, and driving initiatives forward.

Key Elements of Executive Presence:

1. **Confidence in Communication:**
   Executive presence is often most visible in how leaders communicate. Whether presenting to a board of directors or leading a team meeting, leaders with executive presence communicate clearly, confidently, and concisely. They are prepared, anticipate questions, and are comfortable addressing difficult topics head-on.

2. **Composure Under Pressure:**
   In high-stakes situations, executive presence is demonstrated by how well you manage stress and pressure. Leaders who maintain composure—whether in crisis or conflict—project an image of reliability and competence. In Chapter 12, we discussed the importance of navigating disagreement and conflict without losing your cool. This composure builds trust and reassures your team that you can handle challenges.

3. **Body Language and Non-Verbal Cues:**
   How you carry yourself physically plays a significant role in how you're perceived as a leader. Stand tall, make eye contact, and use gestures that convey openness and confidence. People will notice how you move, and these non-verbal cues can either enhance or detract from your leadership presence.

4. **Emotional Intelligence:**
   Leaders with strong executive presence are emotionally intelligent. They understand how to read a room, pick up on non-verbal signals, and adapt their communication style based on their audience. They also have the ability to regulate their own emotions, ensuring that they don't overreact in stressful situations.

Example of Executive Presence in Action: Imagine a senior marketing director presenting a critical project update to the executive team. She speaks clearly, without overloading her audience with unnecessary details. When faced with a tough question from the CFO, she responds calmly and thoughtfully, acknowledging the concern and offering a solution. Throughout the presentation, she maintains eye contact and uses purposeful gestures. Even when a disagreement arises, she remains composed, showing that she can handle pressure. By the end of the meeting, her ability to project confidence and composure ensures that the executive team trusts her judgment and recommendations.

CONCLUSION: BUILDING LEADERSHIP THROUGH CONFIDENCE, ASSERTIVENESS, AND PRESENCE

Leadership presence is not a matter of personality—it's a matter of practice. Whether you're introverted, extroverted, or somewhere in between, you can learn to project confidence, assert yourself in critical moments, and build an executive presence that commands respect. Ultimately, leadership isn't just about the decisions you make, but about how you make those decisions and how you present yourself to others.

In the next chapter, we'll delve into the world of office politics and how to navigate the dynamics of power and influence within organizations to drive your career forward.

Chapter 15:

Office Politics – Playing the Game Ethically

In a hallway where office politics simmer, Robert remains composed and ethical. His integrity serves as a quiet yet firm example for those around him.

INTRODUCTION:
UNDERSTANDING THE UNWRITTEN RULES OF INFLUENCE

For many professionals, the term "office politics" conjures up images of backstabbing, manipulation, and jockeying for power at the expense of others. However, office politics—when understood and navigated ethically—are simply the art of managing influence and power dynamics within an organization. As you climb the leadership ladder, office politics will inevitably play a larger role in your day-to-day life, whether you choose to engage with them or not. The higher you rise, the more complex the power dynamics become.

In this chapter, we'll shift the negative perception of office politics and reframe them as an essential part of leadership. We'll explore how to navigate the political landscape of your organization with integrity, ensuring that you build relationships and position yourself for success while maintaining your values. You'll learn how to build political savvy in a way that fosters trust, shields your team from unnecessary distractions, and ensures that your contributions are recognized without compromising your ethical foundation.

UNDERSTANDING THE UNWRITTEN RULES OF INFLUENCE

As you advance in your career, the decisions that affect your success will increasingly be made in rooms you may not be present in—executive meetings, informal discussions, or high-level strategy sessions. Understanding the power dynamics and unwritten rules of these environments is crucial to positioning yourself and your team for success.

What Are Office Politics? At its core, office politics is about power—who holds it, how it's distributed, and how it's used to influence decisions. It's the informal side of how organizations function, beyond the formal hierarchy. While your job title defines your position in the organizational chart, office politics is about the relationships, networks, and alliances that operate behind the scenes.

Leaders who navigate office politics effectively understand that influence often matters as much, if not more, than formal authority. As you rise in leadership, you'll find that many decisions are not made in a vacuum—they're influenced by relationships, personal dynamics, and competing priorities across the organization. **Office politics are not inherently negative**—they are simply a reality of how organizations function. The key is learning how to engage with them in a way that aligns with your values and goals.

The Increasing Role of Office Politics as You Climb the Ladder

At lower levels in an organization, the focus is largely on individual performance and direct output. As we discussed in Chapter 1 and Chapter 4, early in your career, success is about completing tasks, meeting targets, and demonstrating competency in your role. But as you move into management and senior leadership (Chapters 5 through 10), the nature of success changes. It's no longer just about what you deliver—it's about how you influence others, manage relationships, and ensure your voice is heard when key decisions are being made.

For example, consider how Daniel, now a Vice President, must manage relationships across departments in Chapter 10. His ability to secure resources for his team, influence strategy, and push key initiatives forward depends not just on his expertise, but on the strength of his relationships with senior executives, department heads, and other influential leaders.

As you rise, office politics become less about playing the game to win and more about strategically aligning your actions with the goals of the business and maintaining relationships that allow you to achieve those goals.

ETHICALLY ENGAGING IN OFFICE POLITICS

Navigating office politics ethically means building influence and relationships without compromising your values or engaging in manipulation. Your goal is to foster trust, align your efforts with business goals, and ensure that your contributions are recognized in a way that is both respectful and transparent.

Here's how you can engage ethically in office politics:

1. **Understand Who Holds Influence**

    Every organization has key influencers—people who may not hold the highest titles but whose opinions shape the decisions that are made. These individuals could be senior executives, long-standing employees with deep institutional knowledge, or department heads who wield significant power. Understanding who holds influence in your organization is critical to navigating the political landscape.

    Practical Tip: Start by observing who people turn to for advice or decisions during meetings. Who do senior leaders consult before making significant changes? Building relationships with these influencers will help you better understand how decisions are made and position yourself to contribute meaningfully.

2. **Build Alliances, Not Factions**

    One of the biggest mistakes in office politics is choosing sides too early. Organizations are dynamic, and the power structure can shift over time. Instead of aligning yourself too closely with one group or leader, focus on building a diverse network of allies across the organization. This allows you to remain adaptable and avoid being caught in political crossfires.

    Practical Tip: As discussed in Chapter 12 on networking, be intentional about building relationships across departments and levels. Don't just network with those you perceive as powerful—connect with peers, juniors, and mentors who can provide different perspectives and support your growth.

3. **Position Yourself Based on Value, Not Manipulation**

    Ethical office politics is about positioning yourself for success through the value you bring, not by undermining others or playing manipulative games. Focus on delivering results, aligning your work with the organization's strategic goals, and ensuring that the right people are aware of your contributions.

    Practical Tip: Regularly update your managers and key stakeholders on your team's progress. Frame your contributions in terms of how they impact the broader organization, rather than simply highlighting your personal achievements. This ensures that you're recognized without coming across as self-serving.

4. **Understand Personalities Without Playing to Them**

    Different personalities will influence how you approach relationships in the workplace. Some leaders may respond well to data and logic, while others may be driven by emotions and personal rapport. Understanding these personality dynamics can help you navigate relationships more effectively without feeling like you're being manipulative.

    Practical Tip: Observe how different leaders make decisions. Do they prefer hard data, or are they more influenced by intuition and relationships? Tailor your communication style to meet their needs without compromising your own authenticity.

BUILDING POLITICAL SAVVY WHILE MAINTAINING TRUST

One of the key concerns leaders have about engaging in office politics is the fear of losing trust or being seen as disingenuous. But being politically savvy doesn't mean sacrificing your values—it means navigating relationships thoughtfully, understanding the context in which decisions are made, and ensuring that your contributions are recognized in an ethical way.

1. Build Trust with Key Stakeholders

Trust is the currency of influence. Without trust, even the most politically savvy leaders will find it difficult to navigate office politics successfully. Building trust starts with being transparent, reliable, and authentic in your interactions. When people trust you, they are more likely to support your initiatives, provide you with valuable insights, and advocate for you when you're not in the room.

2. Avoid Gossip and Negative Alliances

One of the quickest ways to lose trust and damage your reputation is by engaging in gossip or forming negative alliances aimed at undermining others. While it can be tempting to join in on office gossip or align yourself with a powerful but divisive figure, these actions can backfire in the long term. Instead, focus on building positive relationships and avoiding office drama.

Example of Trust and Savvy in Action:

Imagine an ambitious director, Megan, who is leading a new initiative within her company. She knows that to secure the resources she needs, she'll have to gain the support of both the CFO, who is data-driven, and the COO, who values relationships and personal rapport. Megan takes time to build trust with both. For the CFO, she presents clear financial projections and data-backed results. For the COO, she spends time building rapport, understanding his goals for the organization, and aligning her project with his vision. By recognizing and navigating these dynamics without sacrificing her own integrity, Megan successfully gains the support she needs to move her initiative forward.

3. Navigate Complex Relationships with Integrity

As you rise in leadership, the relationships you navigate will become more complex. You'll need to manage competing priorities, different personalities, and, sometimes, conflicting agendas. This is where political savvy comes into play—knowing how to balance these dynamics while staying true to your values.

Practical Tip: If you find yourself in a situation where different stakeholders have competing interests, focus on the larger business objectives. Frame your conversations around what's best for the company and how you can align competing priorities to serve that goal. This allows you to maintain neutrality while advancing your own initiatives.

SHIELDING YOUR TEAM FROM OFFICE POLITICS

One of the most important responsibilities you have as a leader is to **shield your team from the distractions of office politics**. While you may need to engage in political navigation at higher levels, your team should not be bogged down by these internal dynamics. Your role is to provide clarity, focus, and stability, ensuring that they can perform at their best without getting caught up in the noise.

1. Keep Political Conflicts at Your Level

When conflicts arise within leadership teams or between departments, it's your responsibility to manage them at your level. Avoid bringing these issues down to your team, where they can create unnecessary distractions or reduce morale. Instead, communicate with your team in a way that keeps them focused on their work and shields them from the complexity of internal politics.

2. Focus Your Team on Shared Goals

One of the best ways to shield your team from office politics is to ensure that they are focused on clear, shared goals. When your team understands what they are working toward and how their work contributes to the larger objectives of the company, they are less likely to be influenced by internal distractions.

Example of Shielding a Team from Politics:
Consider a senior manager, Raj, who is caught between two department heads vying for resources. Raj knows that his team's focus should remain on delivering results, not getting involved in the politics of leadership battles. Rather than letting his team feel the pressure of this conflict, Raj has a candid conversation with his leaders, advocating for his team's resources without pulling them into the fray. He keeps his team focused on their objectives, ensuring that their performance remains high despite the political dynamics above them.

CONCLUSION: PLAYING THE GAME WITH INTEGRITY

Office politics are a reality of leadership, especially as you rise through the ranks. But navigating them ethically, building relationships, and maintaining trust with key stakeholders are essential to ensuring your success without compromising your values. As you grow in your career, your ability to manage political dynamics will define how effectively you lead, how well you can position your team, and how trusted you are within the organization.

By understanding the unwritten rules of influence, building political savvy while maintaining your integrity, and shielding your team from unnecessary distractions, you can navigate office politics in a way that benefits both your career and the organization without ever compromising your ethical foundation.

In the next chapter, we'll explore humility and the idea that "all men are created equal"—how this foundational leadership principle can help you build a culture of respect, inclusivity, and long-term success.

Chapter 16:

Humility – Leading with Empathy and Equality

Sitting with a junior employee in a break room, Robert listens with genuine empathy. His approachable demeanor underscores the humility that defines his enduring leadership.

INTRODUCTION: ALL MEN ARE CREATED EQUAL – THE ROLE OF HUMILITY IN LEADERSHIP

One of the most important realizations in leadership is that **titles do not make you better than others**. The true measure of a leader lies not in the authority they hold but in the humility they carry. Great leaders understand that success isn't about being the smartest or most powerful person in the room—it's about empowering those around you, valuing every team member, and acknowledging that leadership is a privilege, not a pedestal.

This chapter explores how humility shapes leadership. We'll look at the power of admitting when you're wrong, getting comfortable with saying "I don't know," and, most importantly, recognizing that leadership is about enabling others to succeed. Whether you're leading a small team or overseeing an entire organization, humility allows you to connect with people, earn their respect, and create an environment where everyone feels valued.

HUMILITY IN LEADERSHIP: RECOGNIZING THAT YOU DON'T HAVE ALL THE ANSWERS

One of the key turning points in any leader's journey is the moment they realize that they no longer have all the answers—and that's okay. Early in your career, success often comes from being the smartest or most capable person in the room. Your value is measured by your individual contributions, your knowledge, and your ability to solve problems. But as you grow into more senior roles, the demands of leadership change. Your job shifts from being the expert to building a team of experts around you.

Admitting When You're Wrong

A critical part of leadership is the ability to admit when you're wrong. This doesn't undermine your authority—it strengthens it. Admitting mistakes shows that you are human, self-aware, and focused on learning and improving, rather than protecting your ego. Teams respect leaders who own their mistakes, and it sets a powerful example that failure is part of growth.

For example, a senior leader who acknowledges a strategic misstep rather than doubling down on a flawed decision sends a clear message: we learn from our mistakes, and we move forward together. This kind of leadership builds trust because it shows that the leader is focused on the success of the team and the organization, not just their own image.

Saying "I Don't Know"
Equally important is being comfortable saying "I don't know." As you rise in leadership, there will inevitably come a point where you are no longer the subject matter expert. Your role is to attract, hire, and empower people who are smarter or more experienced in specific areas than you are. Instead of feeling threatened by this, embrace it as a strength. The best leaders surround themselves with people who can fill the gaps in their own knowledge.

When a leader admits they don't know the answer to a question, it doesn't weaken their position. It strengthens their ability to find the best solution by seeking input from those who do have the expertise. Saying "I don't know, but let's figure it out together" opens the door to collaboration, innovation, and collective problem-solving.

Example of Humility in Action:
Take the example of Emma, a recently promoted director of product development. In her previous role as a manager, Emma prided herself on knowing every detail of her product lines and guiding her team through every challenge. But in her new role, overseeing multiple teams and product categories, Emma quickly realized that she couldn't

be the expert in every area. Rather than trying to maintain control or pretend she knew everything, she leaned on her team's expertise. She empowered her product managers to make key decisions and wasn't afraid to say, "I don't know, what do you think?" during meetings. By showing humility, Emma built a culture of trust and collaboration, where her team felt valued and respected.

BALANCING CONFIDENCE WITH HUMILITY

One of the most challenging aspects of leadership is balancing **confidence with humility**. Confidence is critical—it's what inspires trust, drives action, and gives your team the assurance that you can lead them through uncertainty. But confidence without humility can quickly turn into arrogance. On the other hand, humility without confidence may make you seem indecisive or weak.

The key is striking the right balance: projecting strength and decisiveness when needed, while also being approachable, self-aware, and open to feedback.

Confidence Is About Direction, Not Ego

Confidence in leadership comes from a place of conviction, not ego. It's about having a clear sense of direction and being able to guide your team toward a common goal. Leaders need to make tough decisions, often with incomplete information. Confidence is what allows you to make those decisions and move forward, even when there is uncertainty.

However, confidence should never close you off from input or make you resistant to change. When combined with humility, confidence becomes a powerful tool for leading teams through challenges. Leaders who are humble enough to admit when they don't have all the answers, but confident enough to act decisively, are the ones who inspire the most trust and loyalty.

Humility Creates Openness to Learning

Humility is the recognition that no matter how far you've come in your career, there's always more to learn. As we discussed in earlier chapters on conflict and decision-making, being open to different perspectives is critical to making informed decisions. Humble leaders seek input from others, recognizing that their own perspective is just one piece of the puzzle.

For instance, in Chapter 13, we discussed how the principle of "disagree and commit" encourages leaders to embrace differing opinions before aligning around a final decision. Humility plays a key role in this process. By being open to feedback and showing a willingness to be challenged, leaders create an environment where team members feel valued and heard.

Example of Balancing Confidence with Humility:

Consider Alex, a VP of sales, who is tasked with making a major strategic decision about entering a new market. He has confidence in his ability to lead the sales team through the transition, but he's also humble enough to acknowledge that he doesn't have all the market data or insight into every potential risk. Instead of pushing forward on his own, Alex brings in experts from the finance and product teams to provide their perspectives. By balancing confidence in his leadership with humility in acknowledging what he doesn't know, Alex is able to make a well-informed decision that benefits the entire organization.

HUMILITY IN ACTION:
EMPOWERING OTHERS AND ELEVATING YOUR TEAM

As you rise in leadership, it's important to realize that your success is no longer about your individual performance—it's about the performance of your team. One of the greatest challenges (and privileges) of leadership is learning to step back and let others shine. Your job is not to be the smartest person in the room; your job is to **attract, hire, train, retain, and empower** the smartest people to do their best work.

Empowering Others to Make Decisions

Humility in leadership means trusting your team to make decisions and giving them the autonomy to execute on their ideas. Micromanagement is often a symptom of insecurity or a need for control, but humble leaders know that true success comes from empowering others to take ownership of their work.

A confident leader who embraces humility provides their team with the resources, tools, and support they need, but doesn't interfere with their process. This not only builds trust but also allows the team to grow and develop their own leadership skills.

Example of Empowering Your Team:

Consider a senior manager who oversees a group of talented engineers. Instead of dictating every decision or insisting on controlling the direction of projects, this leader allows the engineers to take ownership of their work, make key decisions, and drive innovation. By empowering her team to lead in their areas of expertise, the manager fosters an environment of creativity and accountability, where the team feels valued and trusted.

Providing Resources and Context

As a leader, it's also your job to provide the resources and context that your team needs to succeed. This includes access to training, the right tools, and a clear understanding of the company's goals and vision. Humility means recognizing that your team may need support in areas that you're no longer directly involved in, and that's okay.

For example, a CEO who has risen through the ranks of operations might not be familiar with the latest trends in digital marketing. Instead of trying to lead in an area they're not familiar with, they empower the marketing team with the budget and resources needed to succeed. The CEO's humility in recognizing the team's expertise allows the organization to stay competitive in a fast-changing market.

Example of Providing Resources and Support:

In Chapter 7, we discussed how Luis, a senior manager overseeing multiple manufacturing facilities, empowered his plant managers by providing them with the tools and resources they needed to optimize performance. He didn't micromanage their day-to-day operations but trusted them to lead their teams, knowing that they were the experts in their respective areas.

TREATING EVERYONE AS EQUALS: LEADING WITH EMPATHY

At the core of humility is the belief that **we are all equal**, regardless of our roles, titles, or experience. The best leaders know that they are no more valuable than the people they lead. Every person, from the most junior employee to the CEO, brings unique skills, perspectives, and value to the organization.

Recognizing Our Shared Humanity

As leaders, it's important to recognize that no one has it all figured out—not even those at the top. We are all navigating challenges, making mistakes, and learning as we go. Humility helps us understand that leadership is not about perfection or omniscience; it's about being human, embracing vulnerability, and supporting others along the way.

When leaders treat their team members as equals—with respect, empathy, and appreciation—it fosters a culture of collaboration and trust. People feel valued for their contributions, regardless of their title or position, and this sense of equality strengthens the bonds within the team.

Example of Treating Everyone with Respect:
Imagine a department head who takes the time to meet with junior team members, ask for their input, and genuinely listen to their ideas. This leader makes it clear that every voice matters, regardless of title. By treating everyone as equals, the department head fosters a sense of inclusivity and respect, which leads to higher engagement and better team performance.

CONCLUSION: HUMILITY AS THE FOUNDATION OF TRUE LEADERSHIP

Humility is not a weakness—it's the foundation of true leadership. Great leaders understand that their role is not to be the smartest or most powerful person in the room, but to elevate those around them. By admitting when you're wrong, being comfortable with saying "I don't know," and recognizing the value in others, you create an environment where trust, respect, and collaboration thrive.

As you rise in your career, remember that leadership is not about being placed on a pedestal; it's about standing shoulder to shoulder with your team, empowering them to achieve great things together. In the next chapter, we'll explore how to align your personal and professional goals with your leadership journey, ensuring that your values and vision remain at the heart of everything you do.

Epilogue

by Stephen Zimmerman, PhD.

It has been an incredible honor to know Robert Murphy for the past seven years, during which our friendship has grown into a source of inspiration and mutual respect. Robert's boundless creativity, unwavering dedication, and fearless approach to challenging conventional thinking have always impressed me. Being invited to contribute to his newest publication, *Breaking Boundaries*, is not only a testament to our shared vision but also a deeply meaningful opportunity for me. I am thrilled to be part of a project that promises to redefine perspectives and push the limits of innovation, just as Robert has consistently done throughout his remarkable career.

The pages of Breaking Boundaries have taken you on a journey through the diverse stages and forms of leadership, from the early stages of career growth to the upper echelons of executive influence. Leadership is a broad and evolving discipline that defies a single, fixed definition. It transcends titles, formalities, and organizational charts. Instead, leadership is a transformative force that begins with an individual and extends into teams, organizations, and entire industries. As you reach the end of this book, remember that the true end of the journey is not marked by reaching a certain role or level, but by your commitment to growth, service, and positive impact throughout your career.

THE INFINITE LOOP OF LEARNING AND SELF-IMPROVEMENT

One of the fundamental truths about leadership is that it is never complete. Leadership is a dynamic, iterative process that demands continuous growth. Each time you acquire a new skill, overcome a new challenge, or lead a new team, you lay a foundation that can be built upon again. Each new experience adds another dimension to your understanding and expertise, and yet, it also reveals new questions and challenges.

Leadership requires a mindset of lifelong learning and openness to self-improvement. Your journey should be punctuated with moments of introspection, where you pause to assess the distance you have traveled and chart the course ahead. In doing so, you transform leadership from a linear pursuit into a spiral of growth, where each revolution brings new insights, refined skills, and a deeper sense of purpose. Embracing this mindset makes every accomplishment a stepping stone rather than an endpoint, allowing you to see every moment as an opportunity to evolve further.

RESILIENCE: THE CORE OF LASTING LEADERSHIP

Every leader will face obstacles that test their resolve and commitment. These challenges may arise in the form of failures, setbacks, unexpected changes, or difficult decisions. The ability to remain resilient, even in the face of adversity, is what separates those who endure and succeed from those who fall short.

Resilience is not merely about surviving hardship; it's about adapting and thriving because of it. When faced with obstacles, resilient leaders don't back down; instead, they seek to understand the lessons embedded within each experience. They ask themselves questions like, "What can this teach me?" and "How can I use this to become stronger?" By adopting this mindset, you transform each setback into a powerful catalyst for growth and improvement.

But resilience isn't achieved in isolation; it's often a product of supportive environments, both within and beyond the workplace. Building a support network, practicing self-care, and fostering open lines of communication with mentors and peers are all vital. Resilience is reinforced by these connections, reminding us that leadership is not a solitary journey but a collective one. When you cultivate resilience in yourself, you also model it for others, inspiring your team and creating a culture where setbacks are seen not as end-points but as learning moments.

LEADERSHIP AS A TOOL FOR EMPOWERMENT AND SERVICE

Perhaps one of the most overlooked but crucial aspects of leadership is that it is, at its heart, a service. True leadership doesn't seek glory for itself but instead creates opportunities for others to succeed. As a leader, your role is to empower those around you—to help them discover their potential, provide them with the resources and guidance they need to grow, and create a safe environment where they can make mistakes and learn.

Effective leadership is not about accumulating power but about sharing it in a way that benefits the collective. Leaders who focus on service approach their roles with humility, empathy, and a genuine desire to help others succeed. This is the cornerstone of servant leadership, a philosophy that teaches us to lead with empathy and compassion rather than authority and dominance. When you adopt this approach, you'll find that people are not only willing to follow you, but they'll be inspired to go above and beyond because they know they are valued and supported.

Empowering others is about more than merely delegating tasks—it's about giving them the freedom to contribute meaningfully and to see the impact of their work. This means trusting your team, giving them room to innovate, and providing constructive feedback that helps them grow. By focusing on empowerment, you become a multiplier of leadership, enabling others to step up, take ownership, and become leaders themselves.

BUILDING TRUST AND LEADING WITH INTEGRITY

Trust is the currency of effective leadership. Without trust, teams can't function cohesively, innovation stalls, and productivity wanes. But trust doesn't come simply from holding a title—it must be earned through consistency, transparency, and ethical behavior. Leading with integrity means being honest, keeping your promises, and upholding the values that you wish to see in others.

When you lead with integrity, you create an environment where people feel safe to speak up, contribute their ideas, and take risks. Trust builds a foundation for open communication, which is essential for collaboration and innovation. Leaders who inspire trust aren't afraid to be vulnerable, admit their mistakes, or seek input from their teams. By doing so, they model the kind of behavior that encourages others to do the same, creating a culture of transparency and mutual respect.

Furthermore, trust is essential for navigating times of uncertainty or change. In moments of transition, teams look to their leaders for reassurance and stability. When trust is present, your team will have confidence in your vision and be more willing to follow your guidance, even when the path ahead is unclear. This kind of trust is built gradually, over time, through consistent actions that demonstrate your commitment to their well-being and success.

INNOVATION THROUGH DIVERSITY OF THOUGHT AND INCLUSION

Today's work environments are more diverse than ever, encompassing a wide range of backgrounds, experiences, and perspectives. Leaders who understand the value of diversity see it not just as a box to check but as a wellspring of creativity and innovation. By fostering an inclusive environment, you create space for different ideas to flourish, leading to solutions that are richer and more comprehensive.

Diversity of thought is one of the most powerful assets a team can have. When people with different perspectives come together, they bring unique insights and approaches to problem-solving. This can only happen when leaders actively create an environment where everyone feels safe and encouraged to share their ideas. Inclusive leadership isn't about being neutral or passive; it requires a proactive approach to ensuring that all voices are heard, respected, and valued.

By embracing diversity and inclusion, you prepare your team to better understand and respond to the needs of a global, multifaceted marketplace. The best leaders are those who recognize that they don't have all the answers, but they know how to ask the right questions and create a space where answers can emerge from the collective wisdom of the team.

VISION AS A GUIDING COMPASS

A clear, compelling vision is essential to effective leadership. Vision provides direction, motivation, and purpose, enabling both leaders and their teams to stay focused on their goals. But vision is more than a set of words or a lofty ideal; it's a guiding compass that informs every decision and action. Leaders who articulate a powerful vision provide their teams with a sense of purpose, helping them see how their individual efforts contribute to a larger goal.

However, a vision is only as effective as the clarity with which it is communicated. Leaders must be able to convey their vision in a way that resonates with others, turning it from an abstract concept into a shared purpose. This requires consistent, transparent communication and a genuine belief in the vision itself. When people believe in a vision, they're not just working toward it—they're championing it.

Vision also provides a foundation for resilience, enabling teams to remain focused and driven even in challenging times. When leaders can tie daily tasks and short-term goals back to the overarching vision, they inspire a sense of meaning and fulfillment that goes beyond mere productivity. In this way, vision becomes a powerful source of motivation, guiding both the leader and the team through each stage of their journey.

LEADING IN TIMES OF CHANGE AND UNCERTAINTY

The world is in constant flux, and leaders must be prepared to guide their teams through times of change and uncertainty. Whether it's navigating technological disruption, economic shifts, or organizational restructuring, the ability to adapt is crucial. Adaptive leaders approach change with a proactive mindset, anticipating potential challenges and finding ways to turn them into opportunities.

Change is inherently uncomfortable, and it's natural for people to feel uncertain or resistant. Effective leaders help their teams navigate these emotions by maintaining open lines of communication, providing clarity on the reasons for change, and offering support throughout the transition. Adaptive leaders embrace a mindset of flexibility, seeing change not as a disruption but as a catalyst for growth and innovation.

In times of uncertainty, your team will look to you for stability and reassurance. Leading through change means being transparent about what you know and what you don't, acknowledging the challenges, and focusing on the possibilities. Adaptive leaders model resilience, inspire confidence, and create a culture where innovation and flexibility are valued.

LEAVING A LASTING LEGACY

As a leader, the most meaningful legacy you can leave is not the results you achieved or the goals you met, but the people you influenced and the lives you changed. The impact of your leadership will continue to ripple long after you move on, shaping the careers and lives of those you led and mentored. Legacy is about planting seeds that will grow and flourish, even in your absence.

Your legacy is built in the relationships you foster, the values you uphold, and the example you set. It is reflected in the culture you help create and the impact you make on the individuals you lead. Leaders who focus on legacy think not only about the immediate outcomes but about the lasting influence they can have on their teams and organizations. They prioritize the development of others, knowing that true success is not measured by individual achievements but by the growth and success of those they have empowered.

Breaking Boundaries – Your Leadership Journey Ahead

As we come to the end of *Breaking Boundaries*, I hope you've gained valuable insights into the many dimensions of leadership. This book was designed not just to give you tools and strategies, but to help you push beyond the limitations that often hold us back in our careers. Whether it's understanding how to lead with humility, mastering office politics, or building your network with intention, the goal has always been to equip you with the mindset and practices that will allow you to break through boundaries at every stage of your journey.

We started by examining the evolution of leadership roles—from individual contributors just starting out, to mid-level managers, and all the way to senior executives responsible for shaping the future of their organizations. Along the way, we explored the importance of crafting a compelling vision (Chapter 11), developing confidence and presence (Chapter 14), and navigating the often tricky landscape of office dynamics (Chapter 15). Each chapter was designed to show that leadership isn't just about managing people—it's about personal growth, building influence, and making decisions that drive both your career and your organization forward.

RECAP: BREAKING BOUNDARIES THROUGH LEADERSHIP

At the core of this book is the idea that breaking boundaries means growing beyond the limits we often place on ourselves. Whether those boundaries are self-imposed, organizational, or societal, leadership is about constantly pushing past them.

- **In the early chapters**, we discussed how to lay a foundation for success as an individual contributor by taking ownership of your growth, seeking out opportunities to expand your role, and positioning yourself as a leader, even before you have the title.

- **As you progressed into management**, we explored how to lead teams, navigate interpersonal dynamics, and build trust and influence (Chapters 5 through 10). We discussed the shift from focusing on your own performance to empowering your team and leading through others.

- **To close out the book**, we shifted to key leadership principles that apply at every level, covering vision, strategy, conflict resolution, networking, confidence, and humility. These chapters provided essential tools that you can apply throughout your career, regardless of your role.

Throughout each stage, we've talked about how great leaders are those who break through the conventional limits of their roles—by questioning the status quo, learning from failure, and embracing both the challenges and opportunities that come with leadership.

KEEP THIS BOOK HANDY – A REFERENCE FOR EVERY STEP

While *Breaking Boundaries* offers a roadmap for your leadership journey, it's important to remember that leadership itself is an evolving process. The lessons you've learned here are not one-time insights but tools you can revisit again and again as your career progresses. Whether you find yourself preparing for a new leadership role, navigating a difficult team dynamic, or rethinking your personal leadership style, I encourage you to keep this book close by as a reference.

Use it as a reminder to challenge yourself, break past your current limitations, and lead with intention. Leadership is a journey, not a destination—and at every step, you'll face new boundaries to break.

THANK YOU FOR JOINING ME ON THIS JOURNEY

Thank you for purchasing *Breaking Boundaries*. I truly appreciate your trust in me as a guide along your leadership path. This book is a companion to my previous work, *Leadership with a Purpose*, where we explored how to find your place as a leader and how to navigate leadership challenges with intentionality. In *Breaking Boundaries*, I've taken that journey further, focusing on helping you push past limitations and embrace leadership with both confidence and humility.

Leadership is not a solitary journey. It's about the connections we build, the people we inspire, and the impact we leave behind. And so, I want to remind you: you don't have to do it alone.

SHARE YOUR FEEDBACK AND HELP OTHERS BREAK BOUNDARIES

My hope is that this book provides you with insights, tools, and strategies to navigate your leadership journey and inspire growth—both personally and professionally.

Leadership, at its core, is about connection, and feedback is one of the most powerful ways to foster that connection. Whether it's guiding a team or helping someone improve, constructive feedback is a form of leadership that drives progress. Now, I'd like to ask for your feedback.

If this book resonated with you, consider leaving a review on Amazon, Goodreads, or LinkedIn, or simply sharing it with your friends and colleagues. Your perspective not only helps me grow as an author but also guides others who are looking to take control of their careers and break through their own boundaries.

Your voice matters. By sharing your thoughts—what you found valuable, what inspired you, or even areas you'd like to see explored further—you help create a community of learners and leaders striving for growth. Together, we can continue to elevate the conversation about leadership and career progression.

Thank you for your time, your insights, and your leadership in helping others discover *Breaking Boundaries*. Let's keep inspiring one another to push limits and achieve more.

About the Author:

Robert D. Murphy

Throughout this book, I've shared lessons learned over the course of my career about what it truly means to lead. Leadership, as I've discovered, is far more about people than it is about technology. While my journey began as an engineer, immersed in the intricacies of technical work, I soon realized that my passion lay in building and leading teams. Over the past two decades in the tech industry, I've had the privilege of guiding engineering organizations of all sizes—ranging from agile startups to expansive, global enterprises. Along the way, one principle has consistently proven true: people don't leave jobs; they leave managers.

In my earlier book, *Leadership with a Purpose: Motivating Your Engineers*, I explored how leaders can create environments where engineers feel empowered to thrive. *Breaking Boundaries* builds on that foundation, going beyond the technical to focus on the nuanced art of career progression. This book reflects my belief that advancing in your career isn't just about delivering results—it's about creating value for your organization, earning trust, and positioning yourself for growth. From individual contributor to senior leader, I've navigated the challenges of scaling operations, managing complex infrastructures, and fostering cultures rooted in trust, collaboration, and accountability.

Drawing on my experiences leading global teams and working across diverse industries and cultures, *Breaking Boundaries* offers strategies to help readers overcome personal and professional barriers to growth. It's a guide for those looking to navigate the complexities of leadership, career advancement, and influence, and it provides actionable insights for breaking through to the next level of their careers.

As this book concludes, I hope it leaves you inspired to think beyond your current role, take control of your professional future, and approach your career as a journey of continuous growth. Leadership is about making a lasting impact—not just for yourself, but for those you lead and the organizations you serve. My aim is that the strategies and stories shared here empower you to break through your boundaries and achieve the success you envision.

LET'S CONNECT – I'M HERE TO CELEBRATE YOUR SUCCESS

I'm always eager to hear from readers and connect with fellow leaders. If you'd like to stay in touch, please don't hesitate to connect with me on LinkedIn. I'd be honored to celebrate your successes, answer any questions, and continue the conversation. Whether it's a promotion, a leadership challenge, or simply breaking through a boundary in your own career, I'd love to hear how you're applying the insights from this book.

SCAN THE QR CODE TO CONNECT WITH ME ON LINKEDIN.

Leadership is a constant journey of growth, reflection, and action. As you continue breaking boundaries, remember that the best leaders are those who never stop learning, never stop evolving, and never stop empowering those around them. I wish you continued success on your path—and I'm excited to see where your leadership journey takes you.

www.ingramcontent.com/pod-product-compliance
Lightning Source LLC
Chambersburg PA
CBHW051834090426
42736CB00011B/1793